The. Best. Relationship.
Ever.

The. Best. Relationship. Ever.

Wayne C. Allen

2013

© 2013 Wayne C. Allen, M.Th.

The Phoenix Centre Press
55 Northfield Drive, Suite 324
Waterloo, Ontario, Canada 2K 3T6

email: waynecallen@gmail.com
website: http://www.phoenixcentre.com

**Library and Archives Canada
Cataloguing in Publication**

Allen, Wayne Charles, 1951 –

The. Best. Relationship. Ever.
ISBN 978-0-9877192-3-2

1. Relationships 2. Self Actualization

All rights reserved. No part of this book may be reproduced or utilized in any form, or by any means, mechanical or electronic,
including photocopying, recording or by any information storage or retrieval system, without written permission from the publisher.

Disclaimer

The contents of this book are solely the opinion of the author and should not be considered as a form of therapy, advice, direction and/or diagnosis or treatment of any kind: medical, spiritual, mental or other. If expert advice or counseling is needed, services of a competent professional should be sought. The author and the Publisher assume no responsibility or liability and specifically disclaim any warranty, express or implied, as regards this book. The purchaser or reader assumes responsibility for the use of this book.

Thanks and Dedication

I really wanted to thank a few people who have helped me out with my writing career. Writing the book is not, for me, much of an issue. My poor little head is just filled with all kinds of words!

Editing, however, is another story altogether.

Debashis Dutta and the lovely Darbella MacNaughton (see below) have been editing me since *This Endless Moment* came out in 2005. Joining the editor's circle this time 'round was Krystina Pinnau. Each of them came up with clever additions, ideas, and caught my bone-headed typing mistakes. Thanks!

I also want to say a word of thanks and gratitude to Ben Wong and Jock McKeen – friends of the heart, and 2 guys who see the world similarly to me. No. Really. They've been inspirations and role models.

And, as with every book, a dedication to Darbella MacNaughton. Dar and I have known each other since 1982, and have been partners since 1983. I still can't figure out why she puts up with me and my numerous foibles, but she does.

I am so grateful for her love, compassion, and just plain loveliness that my heart hurts. She's one in a million, and she hangs out with me!

And finally, to you, my loyal readers. You read my blog, buy my books, and say nice things. Always. I am so blessed to have you in my life. I am pleased and honoured to walk with you all.

Warmly, Wayne

Other books by Wayne C. Allen

Available on Amazon as Paperbacks, and for Kindle:

Half Asleep in the Buddha Hall

Wayne's "Eastern" book takes you by the hand and leads you to Zen-based peace of mind. *Half Asleep in the Buddha Hall* is a Zen based guide to living life fully and deeply. Using Zen stories old and new, as well as other illustrations and exercises, Wayne C. Allen takes you on an adventure into the uncharted territory of yourself.

This Endless Moment

Worthwhile change comes at a price. If you're tired of the same old relationships, the same situations cropping up again and again, and you find yourself stuck in the middle, then right now, you can do something about it! It's time to decide!

If you are willing to commit to living the life you have dreamed of, surrounded by meaningful and deep relationships, while making a real difference in the world, you need *This Endless Moment*.

Find Your Perfect Partner

You've likely realized that the screwy relationships you have been in were the direct result of not thinking about how to create an excellent one. Pretending the important, life-altering decision to relate is "a matter of the heart" is not only stupid, it doesn't work! **Find Your Perfect Partner** is a guide to figuring out the whole attraction / dating / relationship thing.

Contents

INTRODUCTION — 1

CHAPTER ONE: WHY YOU FAIL AT RELATING — 5

A beginner's guide to screwing up — 5
  1. Magical Thinking — 5
  2. Trying to Avoid Conflict — 11
  3. Power Plays – making demands — 12
  4. Story-telling and Drama — 14
  5. Manipulation — 15
  6. Confusion about feelings – sex, charge, microdots — 16
  7. Betrayal — 22
  8. Playing games – Unspoken (Hidden) Intent — 26

Failing at Communication — 27
  Problem: About vs. At — 28
  Problem: Protected vs. Open — 29
  Problem: Sensitivity vs. Insensitivity — 30

CHAPTER TWO: A CASE STUDY IN WEIRD RELATING — 34

The Ballad of Sally and Sam — 34
  Sexual Patterning — 35
  The Triggering Event — 37
  I suggested to Sally and Sam a better way of relating — 41
  Elegant relating has no judgement connected to it — 42

CHAPTER THREE: A NEW MODEL FOR RELATING — 44
  The crux of Elegant, Intimate Relating — 46
  Elegant, Intimate Relating is All about Intent — 48

The key to elegant relating is dialogue — 49
  Integrity holds it all together — 53

Curiosity and Acceptance	54

CHAPTER FOUR: TOOLS FOR RELATING   57

Elegant, Intimate Relating (EIR)   57
    The Beginning of Elegant, Intimate Relating   59
    This becomes the framework for Engaged Intimacy   60

The 9 Tools   60
    1. Total Honesty   62
    2. Being Present   63
    3. Being self-responsible   63
    4. Speaking clearly - Use dialogue to know yourself   64
    5. Being Curious – and NODing   65
    6. Letting go of Drama and Storytelling   65
    7. Being Flexible   66
    8. Feeling Your Feelings   67
    9. Exploring Sensuality and Sexuality   68

CHAPTER FIVE: TOTAL HONESTY   70

    About Total Honesty, and why you need to adopt it   70

CHAPTER SIX: BEING PRESENT   75

CHAPTER SEVEN: BEING SELF-RESPONSIBLE   84

CHAPTER EIGHT: SPEAKING CLEARLY - USING DIALOGUE TO KNOW YOURSELF   94

    The difference between a feeling and an interpretation   96

  All About Action   102

The elements of the Communication Model	103
Dialogue Examples	107

CHAPTER NINE: BEING CURIOUS – AND NODING
109

CHAPTER TEN: LETTING GO OF DRAMA AND STORYTELLING
117

CHAPTER ELEVEN: BEING FLEXIBLE
123

CHAPTER TWELVE: FEELING YOUR FEELINGS 131

Ways to Express Emotions	136
Learning to Feel Your Feelings	136
Expressing Anger	138
Releasing Anger	140
Anger Variation	141
And Another – The pillow push	141
Lastly, Hand Pushing	142
Expressing Grief	142
Adding a cradling	144
Finding Joy	145
More Practice in Feeling what you Feel	146

CHAPTER THIRTEEN: EXPLORING SENSUALITY AND SEXUALITY
149

Vulnerability Projects	156
Erotic Vulnerability Projects	157
Establish an Erotic Vulnerability Project	157
Dialogues about Sexuality	158
About Attraction and Physical Contact with Others	162
Discussing Attraction / Microdots	164

CHAPTER FOURTEEN: EXERCISES IN ELEGANT, INTIMATE RELATING — 167

Exercise # 1 – First Essay – Stages of Relating — 168
Exercise # 2 – Setting Aside Time — 170
Exercise # 3 – Resolving Issues — 172
Exercise # 4 – Viewing another's World — 173
Exercise # 5 – Implement a 'caring days' list — 174
Exercise # 6 – Establish a 'date night' — 176
Exercise # 7 – Be sure you've set up a safe area for expressing emotions — 177
Exercise # 8 – Essay 2 – write about your greatest fears — 177
Exercise # 9 – Silent sitting and eye-gazing — 178
Exercise # 10 - Review the state of your relationship, and make a new commitment — 178

CHAPTER FIFTEEN: SENSUAL, EROTIC EXERCISES — 180

Opening to Passion — 181
  Back Release — 181
  A yoga posture — 181
  Intentional Dancing — 182

Sensuality Exercises — 183
  Belly Breathing — 183
  Cuddling — 184
  Non-erotic, Sensual Massage — 184
  Four-handed massage — 185
  Practice full body hugging — 185
  Practice hugging friends — 186
  The Sitting Hug — 187
  Eat a Rolo ® — 187
  Be a Captive – Full Body Feeling — 188

Exercises in Eroticism — 189

Erotic Massage	189
Learning to Feel and Move Energy	192
The Yab Yum Posture	193
Erotic four-handed Massage	195
Sexuality	**195**
Sexual Healing	195
Yab Yum, level 4	196

CHAPTER SIXTEEN: REFLECTION – WHAT'S NEXT   197

Final Thoughts   200

RESOURCES   202

Introduction

First of all, welcome!

My wife Darbella (Dar for short) and I have been developing and teaching Elegant, Intimate Relating since we met in 1982. We've helped hundreds of clients to strengthen and deepen their relationships. Needless to say, what you're about to read is the bedrock for our own relationship.

We'd like to help you – if you use what we've learned, your relationship will become the best is can be.

Over the years, I've written two booklets about relating[1], as well as creating "The List of 50," a method to figure out what you want in a partner (expanded to a full length book, Find Your Perfect Partner.[2]) Recently, I decided it was time for a practical guide on Elegant, Intimate Relating (EIR)… a book designed to help you to learn to be the best you can be in your relationship.

The. Best. Relationship. Ever. teaches the nuts and bolts of building and maintaining a great relationship. You'll learn what Elegant, Intimate Relating looks like, you'll discover how to communicate with clarity and curiosity, and you'll discover how to continue deepening your relationship over time.

---

[1] http://www.phoenixcentre.com/free_for_the_asking.htm
[2] http://www.phoenixcentrepress.com/getting-exactly/exactly/

The. Best. Relationship. Ever.

The Plot Thickens

The best gift you can give yourself, right now, is an acknowledgment – your past experiences with relating have been less than stellar. You really don't know what it takes to create a relationship that soars.

And really, why would you? They're pretty rare. Most experts, including me ;-) figure that only 5% of the population ever figures this one out.

That's why so many people divorce; that's why so many others have dull, boring relationships.

Hard Work is Required

Fair warning: Elegant, Intimate Relating is a long and winding road. I want to be clear. This book has no short-cuts – just plain speaking, and hard work.

Relationship work is personal and individual

Now, that may seem a bit odd in a book titled, **"The. Best. Relationship. Ever."** I'm stating it this way to make a point. Despite the fact that the number of people in a traditional relationship is two, there is only one person that can change how you relate to your partner. You!

Therefore, not one suggestion in this book is aimed at your partner. This book is not a tool to change your partner! This book is designed to get you to stop looking outside of yourself, either for rescue, or to blame. You'll learn to take responsibility and ownership for your part, and *only your part*, of what happens in the relationship.

Have a look at the relationship you are in (or the one that just ended!) Now, say after me:

Introduction

"I created this. Every aspect of my life is just as it is, and it is as it is because of how I think, and what I do. Waiting for my partner to change is silly, as the only person I have a chance of changing is me. So, here I go – from this point on, I am claiming total responsibility for how I see myself, and what I choose to do."

There! Don't you feel all warm and fuzzy inside?

We're going to go on a walk into 100% self-responsibility. By the end of this book, you'll know whether there's a chance in hell to save your current relationship (hint: there is, but not easily, as there's a ton of water under that bridge, and doing things differently requires strenuous effort.)

If your latest relationship has tanked, then reading this book may just make your next relationship soar.

In either case, you must keep your nose on your side of the fence, learn and implement what this book teaches – a new way of being in the world – and get over yourself.

The. Hardest. Rule. Ever.

I say this to my clients, first session, and often in the first 10 minutes:

"The hardest thing to accept is this idea – everything, 100%, that is going on inside of you is caused by you. Others do not "make you feel" – they don't create your internal experience. That's you in there, doing all of it. Therefore, everyone else is off the hook."

The only way another person can affect us is *physically* – someone with a gun can "make you" do stuff. Someone *verbally* demanding that you do something has absolutely no power over you.

The. Best. Relationship. Ever.

Similarly, others do not make you happy, sad, angry, bored, or turned on. What you feel is you, choosing.

This is the "make or break understanding" for having a meaningful life and for **The. Best. Relationship. Ever.**

Please note! If you are working on a current relationship, it is best if you and your partner read this book concurrently, and discuss it as you go. Toward the end are lots of exercises for practicing what you learn, and being "on the same page" is the only way to practice, learn, and incorporate the new understandings.

- OK, so the plan is to share some essential concepts, and look at how relationships fail.
- Then, a case study, featuring Sam and Sally.
- We'll look at Elegant, Intimate Relating.
- I'll then give you tools for Elegant, Intimate Relating, so that you too can have *The*. Best. Relationship. Ever.

Let's go for the ride. Read carefully, absorb what you read, and experiment with the exercises. This stuff doesn't happen by magic. You actually have to implement it!

Note:

Use of the single quote: many words in this book are enclosed in 'single quotes.' These are terms that are worth noticing.

Example: The word 'wise.' Consider this word's meaning. Is there, really, a definition of 'wise' that we all agree on, or is the matter of 'wisdom' entirely subjective? Does 'wise' not mean what I mean it to mean?

Chapter One:
Why You Fail at Relating

A beginner's guide to screwing up

Before we can begin to talk about how to develop and nourish a deep and meaningful relationship, we'd best get a handle on some of the ways people screw up.

Here is a short list of beliefs that get in the way of having **The. Best. Relationship. Ever.** In no particular order:

- Magical Thinking
- Trying to Avoid Conflict
- Power Plays – making demands
- Story-telling and Drama
- Manipulation
- Confusion about feelings – sex, charge, intimacy
- Betrayal
- Playing Games – Unspoken Intent

1. Magical Thinking

When I'm talking with clients, I usually blame Hollywood, tongue in cheek, for relationship issues.

The. Best. Relationship. Ever.

TV and movies have painted a picture about relating that is both unreal and impossible to achieve. We see a glimpse of a story, and think, "I want a relationship like that!" And then, we concoct a picture in our heads (the movie in our heads) starring our perfect partner. The movie rivals Hollywood in its magic and special effects.

Then, we go out and try to fill the starring role with a real person, and fail. We fail because of Magical Thinking.

The main themes of Magical Thinking are:

- rescue by a Fairy Godmother (or some other magical being, like god)
- a noble knight and his horse, riding to the rescue, or the sudden appearance of a compliant Princess
- magic (spells, affirmations, "The Secret," etc.)
- living happily ever after, with no work , no drama, and no crisis
- quests – by searching long and hard, you will find your "Sleeping Beauty or Prince Charming"

These themes and others reoccur in most popular media, and typically follow the plot line of: boy meets girl, boy loses girl, boy defeats the bad guys / evil monster / the "other man," boy re-captures girl, AND they live happily ever after.

We live and breathe this stuff. Hollywood feeds us more, but we have a choice about whether we *consume* the dream.

Even though most of us can tell truth from fiction, the pull of magical relationship thinking can short-circuit our brains. You sense it when something goes wrong. That tightness in your chest and gut is the, "This can't be happening to me!" sensation, and it's based on the magical idea, "If I'm with the 'right' person, everything will just work."

Here's my favourite example. I once had a female client who was married to "Peter Pan." The guy had a Ph.D., and was a professor. He didn't come for therapy very often, as I challenged his magical thinking – he called me "buzz kill" – in a sense, I was raining on his fantasy parade.

Here's what he said about his wife, his marriage, and his fantasy relationship: "I know for a fact that my wife is not my soul mate. She's a nice person to live with while I wait to meet my soul mate. I have been in many, many relationships, but none have worked out, because I never found my soul mate. Even though I am now married, I am still looking for her." (Hint to Peter Pan: You can't find her; she lives in Never-Never Land!)

Scratching my head, I asked, "How will you know your soul mate when you meet her; how will the relationship differ from your many previous relationships?"

He replied, "She will be beautiful and completely focussed on making me happy. There will never be any conflict, disagreement, or problems. We will live a life of complete personal, relational, and sexual bliss."

I was glad I was not drinking coffee, or it would have shot out of my nose. One more snippet: this guy was nearing 60 at the time.

The kicker? He went off for a holiday (alone) and thought he met his soul mate. He came home and asked his wife for 'permission' to go back to the island in the sun (no, really!) there to spend 30 idyllic days discovering if she truly was his soul mate. My client agreed to take him back if things didn't work out, (no one said clients make sense...) and off he went.

His "soul mate" ended up being a dominatrix, and he came home whipped (literally) and hairless (another story al-

The. Best. Relationship. Ever.

together.) He sighed, and said, "I was so sure, but having to wear a dog collar was the deal breaker."

Yet, at last report, 5 years later, he's still looking.

Peter Pan, in spades.

Magic is in the mind

Many adults believe in soul mates, and that:

- true love *just happens*,
- everyone is entitled to their very own prince(ss,)
- 'true' relationships "work on auto-pilot," have no conflicts, and are "easy sailing."

So tell me, do you see a lot of relationships like that, other than on the Silver Screen?

None-the-less, we watch the movies, and create a movie in our heads. It features our ideal partner (I call this person the "imaginary friend") – a person so perfect as to defy logic. We endow the fantasy person, *and the fantasy relationship,* with all of the magical qualities just listed.

We then go searching for someone to match our "imaginary friend." Well, yikes – this person doesn't exist, and the movies in our heads aren't real.

I also call Magical Thinking the Fallacy of Romance

Romance is driven by hormones. You meet someone, and chemistry happens! Brain chemistry, hormones, endorphins kick in – and if the person even superficially matches your imaginary friend, you fall into lust. You want more, more, more! As the song goes,

Why You Fail at Relating

> *Love is the drug, got a hook on me.*
> *Oh, oh, catch that buzz.*
> *Love is the drug I'm thinking of.*
> *Oh, oh, can't you see,*
> *Love is the drug for me. – Roxy Music*

You could say that you 'love' the feeling, and that you use the person to create the buzz.

- Because of the addictive nature of lust, the person you are enamoured with is turned into the *"object* of my affection."
- Love, we read, is *rosy* – as in seeing through rose-coloured glasses.
- Love is blind – or perhaps better, love is blind to the actual person – your mind is fixated on its fantasy, "imaginary friend," which you attempt to project outward onto the real person.

You've lost that lovin' feeling (The Righteous Brothers)

This happens, every time. This is the point where the fog of lust dissipates enough for you to see the actual person you are in relationship with. Right there! Next to you in bed, and (s)he has morning breath.

For most, there is a bit of panic. Up into our heads we pop, as we try to make sense of what just happened. There are a couple of choices:

- The adult, the mature person, thinks: "Whoa! Where the hell was I? Man, was I ever caught up in lust. Those are some powerful drugs! Am I ever glad I woke up. Now I can decide if I want to work on a real relationship with this real person, lying right here, next to me."
- The vast majority (quasi-adults) think, "This person is no longer living up to my expectations!" Which is shorthand

The. Best. Relationship. Ever.

for, "(S)he isn't behaving according to my fantasy." And the manipulation, games, and strategies start, as you try to force the person in bed to conform to your story.

Magical Thinking actually explains a lot of our silly beliefs

Because we have a fantasy that life should be fair, and that I should 'win,' we have trouble with anything that goes 'wrong.' Magical thinking declares that things are supposed to go the way we want them to. Like Peter Pan, above, we expect that everything will work out, without effort, or with minimal effort. We think we've been cheated when it doesn't.

Rather than challenging the magical thinking, we get caught up in the drama of blaming others, our parents, or God – we blame them that our fantasy isn't magically made real!

And yet, the world is operating another way altogether. That way is this:

What happens, happens. What is, is. If you do not like life now, wait a minute, have a breath, do something different, and you'll likely see something else. And most importantly, the cosmos does not have you (Ego-you) in mind, does not care one way or another what happens to you, and will tick quite merrily long after you are dead and gone.

The cosmos is not a vending machine, into which you insert your wishes and desires, and out of which pops what you want. Sorry.

Take away point:

The bottom line is that the more you fantasize, and the more you get upset that your fantasies aren't coming true, the less you live in the present. Life goes on, and you're stuck in fantasy and frustration.

Your fantasies are only 'real' to you – the stories you tell yourself are crafted by you to prove whatever point you are making. Until you learn to let go of your fantasy world and live in the 'real' one, you are doomed to unhappiness.

*People are who they enact – I am, always & only, **what I do**.*

To repeat, what goes on in your head is neither 'real,' not 'true.' It's a cleverly constructed illusion, created by you, starring you, following your plot devices. You can't stop story making, but you can stop taking it seriously.

2. Trying to Avoid Conflict

When confronted with our partner's demands that we act like their "imaginary friend," we might, initially, give it a try. We do this to keep the peace.

At first, it all seems so reasonable. Our partner is asking for "little changes," and love is all about giving, right? So, it's easier, in the short term, to give *in*.

Even though we are taught that "Love is kind," and that compromise is good, a problem arises when we endlessly pretend to be someone other than who we. Eventually, we become uncomfortable. And another problem: giving in leads to... wait for it... more giving in!

My newest client said, "For seven years, I've done everything he wanted me to. I changed how I dress, spoke, acted. I made his lunches, and called him several times a day to tell him I love him. This time, when he left, he said I was smothering him."

• • •

The. Best. Relationship. Ever.

I suspect she gave up more than 50% of her personality, and repressed her own desires regarding how she wanted to live her life. And even after all of that "giving in," she still couldn't make him happy.

Well, of course not!

When he compares her to his "imaginary friend," my client always comes up short. She can't "make" him happy. Happiness, like everything else, is an inside job.

Take away point:

The. Best. Relationship. Ever. *requires that 2 adults show up, and be who they are. It's not about performing endlessly pleasing behaviours – all that gets you is demands for more of the same. (My client said, "I thought if I was nice to him, he'd want to give me what I needed. In 7 years he never did.")*

This book is all about bringing you – all of you – to the party. By using such things as total honesty and elegant communication, you end up engaging in Elegant, Intimate Relating. You know yourself, and are endlessly curious about your partner.

3. Power Plays – making demands

Another big problem is the "parent - child" relationship. One partner is endlessly trying to 'fix' the other. Lots of sighing, finger-pointing, name calling.

Here's an example: Sam and Sally waltz into the office. Sally is leading. Sally talks... a lot. Sam listens... and nods. Sally is a rising star, a professional. Sam is self-employed, and struggling.

Sally: "Now Sam, you know that you promised to be home on time, and dear knows I don't ask much of you, but how can you expect me to be happy to see you when you're late, and

Why You Fail at Relating

you don't even call to tell me, and a considerate person would call, and it never used to be this way!" (Big breath, sniffle.)

Sam: "Oh... well... it's not that bad... and besides, I'm out on calls in the wilderness and there's no phone."

Sally: "We've been over and over this, and you just don't realize that I worry about you, and I've cooked dinner, except for the two times last week I stayed late at the office, (without telling him, of course...) and if you loved me you'd do this one little thing for me." (Breath, choked-off-sob.)

Sam: "Well... I know you're upset, but I do love you... and well... I really..."

Sally: "That's what you always say!"

I said: "What about a car phone?" (This happened "back in the day" when having a cell phone was rare, and they were huge...)

Sally: "What? Well, I suppose... I'm not sure... Well..."

Sam: (all excited...) "Sure, we could do that."

Two weeks later, they return, same entrance routine.

Sally: (to me) "Fine idea that was. It didn't work at all."

Sam: "Now Sally. I did too call. In fact, I called 8 times out of 10 workdays."

Sally: "That's what I mean. I just can't depend on you. It's really upsetting when you don't call. Now you've gone and missed two times! I made dinner and I worry about you..."

I pointed out to Sally that 8 out of 10 was a pretty big step forward. Sally looked at me as if I had horns. By the next session, though, she'd completely dropped the "You never call" routine and replaced it with "Sam never picks up the trash."

Sally has a lot invested in three things:

- That Sam is not behaving correctly,
- That Sam should do it her way, because she's right, and

The. Best. Relationship. Ever.

- That she is destined to play the tragic heroine, mothering error-prone Sam until the day he dies. Sally placed all the blame for the failure of the relationship on Sam – and she could not see that she created issues out of thin air.

Take away point:

A relationship is not a power play. It's not about lectures, demands, and definitely is not about 'fixing' the other person. It is about becoming elegant and efficient about resolving issues as they occur, without blaming.

4. Story-telling and Drama

One of the things I've noticed over the years is that our stories change to fit our preconceived notions, and therefore have very little to do with either 'truth,' or 'reality.'

Stories mostly get in the way. What I mean is that when I'm in storytelling mode, I'm much more interested in convincing my partner of the validity of my story than I am in resolving issues, coming up with alternatives, or even caring much about the other person. I am invested in having her see 'my way' and that 'my way is right.' Then, because she doesn't see things 'my way' I tell myself that she doesn't care for me. Quite the story.

The more energy I invest in defending my story, the more I'm locked into being right.

Stories do serve a purpose – they are used to validate an idea – but are often misused to excuse and justify refusing to alter my life.

Drama is Similar

Drama adds in awfulizing and universalizing – the situation is declared to be the worst, the most complicated, never-ending horror on the planet – and it's happening to me, poor me – again!

Drama steals our ability to be sane, rational, and present. Drama parallels storytelling in that it distracts us from the only thing that's important – resolving the present moment situation. And, of course, drama is entertaining!

Take away point:

You need to understand that your stories and drama are just diversions, and living your life in their thrall means no depth to your relationships. Period. In other words, there is what is happening, and your story about what is happening.

Add in drama, and the story becomes much larger than the original event. (You see that in the Sam and Sally story, above.) The way out is to acknowledge our stories and dramas, and then let them go. We can then resolve the actual (quite small in comparison) issue.

5. Manipulation

Manipulation is all about using subtle word games to get another to change. I'm giving it special air time because it's presented as "being helpful," or "having my partner's interest at heart." Power plays are obvious and aggressive, while manipulation is subtle and passive aggressive.

"If you love me, you'll do this one little thing for me" is a manipulative statement. The implication is that a demand couched in love and defined as "little" will be easier to swallow.

The. Best. Relationship. Ever.

Manipulative people have a hard time understanding why love doesn't equate with getting exactly what they want.

And the odd piece is that it's never reciprocal – it would never occur to the manipulator to accept the same "little suggestions" from their partner.

Take away point:

Manipulation is a game. It's designed to back one's partner into a soft corner, and to get something "just because." The problem is that manipulation is not even close to dialogue, where options are explored and both parties are heard. Just because it's coy and gentle doesn't make it any less damaging to the relationship.

6. Confusion about feelings – sex, charge, microdots

This will be a long section, as sexual matters are confusing for many people. Let's look at a few issues:

Charge

Let's define charge as, "An internal vibration of pleasurable energy that is both self-referential and driven to repeat itself."

Self-referential: Charge is chargy, and is caused by *internal* factors – it is caused by itself – chargy energy is one form of your life energy.

Remember the 100% rule – what happens inside of you is completely about you. No one can 'make' you feel good, turned on, unhappy, or angry. How your energy flows is all about you – you choose your reaction – including whether you are going to "feel the charge."

Why You Fail at Relating

Driven to repeat: The free flow of energy feels 'good,' and we therefore want more of it. Misunderstanding the game, we tend to link internal with external. We think the external event or person caused the charge, so we keep repeating the external experience, as opposed to going inside and making more charge.

I see this in Bodywork, all the time. I'll be working on, say, a client's shoulders and jaw, and her pelvis will suddenly start moving. If she lets herself continue to move her pelvis, I'll hear, "Wow! What's that? I feel sooo... good!" What she's feeling is a blockage (in the neck/throat) going away, and an immediate rush or flow of energy. If she's wise, she'll understand that the energy is hers – and she's "going with the flow."

Others can facilitate my process – they don't create it

To state it again: Charge is tricky. Most people have externalized it, and then blame their partner if the sensation diminishes. "You just don't turn me on any more!" Well, (s)he never did. You turn yourself on, you turn yourself off. Lack of charge is internal and always about boredom and choosing not to create variety.

The stupid choice is to change "dance partners," or add one in (have an affair,) because this follows the erroneous belief that others create charge in us.

Take away point:

Charge is an internal process, and you can learn to re-charge yourself at will. You have been conditioned to believe that external situations and especially people 'cause' your charge, but it "ain't necessarily so." In every case, the level of charge I feel is only as much as I am letting myself feel. If you want more charge in your life, you'll need to give yourself permission

The. Best. Relationship. Ever.

to feel more charge, in more places. You'll have to stop limiting your "charge experiences" to the socially accepted ones.

And no, I'm not contradicting myself. You have a list of 'acceptable' people, places, and ways of letting yourself feel charge. The feeling of charge is not caused by the people, places, and ways – it is caused by your stories (pre-determined) about where feeling charge is OK. If you want more, you need to re-write your script to include more opportunities for yourself, and then release your physical blocks to chargy-ness. Like everything else, it's all about you!

You'll also discover as we go along that charge has many modes of expression – it can be expressed through sensuality, eroticism – not just through sexual arousal.

Microdots

My buddies Ben Wong and Jock McKeen, retired founders of The Haven, Gabriola Island, B.C., developed and polished this concept. They define a microdot this way:

In a similar fashion [to an encoded film microdot...], the aspects of the "perfect partner" are condensed and encoded; when people meet someone, they can subconsciously check off that individual's attributes against the checklist of the internal microdot. This explains the specificity of the sexual charge.

Discovering your microdot is as simple as paying attention to yourself. Just go to a place where people watching is common (say a Mall, or the beach, etc.) and have a seat and watch. You'll notice that you find some people attractive, some neutral, and some not attractive.

Every now and again, an interesting thing will happen. Someone will go by that "snaps your head around." You are immediately drawn to the person, and the feeling is one of intense sexual attraction and sexual interest.

Now, you may choose to disregard or block actually noticing this reaction. In fact, if you are in a committed relationship, you've likely trained yourself to pretend that you have no such sexually driven interest in others.

I suppose you could continue to believe this, but it is not true. We are attracted to some people, repelled by others, and indifferent to most. And each of us, like it or not, has a microdot pattern. Noticing it, I can play with it, and not take it too seriously.

There is something hard wired and chargy about microdots. The attraction is physical, sexual, and visceral. So, acts of sensuality and sexuality between microdots are "off the hook."

You just don't want to marry your microdot

Why? Because, typically, the sexual attraction will be all the relationship has going for it, and everything else will be conflict and mis-communication. This is because a microdot connection has everything to do with hormones, visual cues, etc. and nothing to do with core issues. See my book, *Find Your Perfect Partner* [1] for more on this!

Take away point:

Microdots remind us of how chargy and delicious a sexual charge is. They also remind us, if we are wise, that sexual attraction, and even good sex, is indicative of absolutely nothing. It does not indicate compatibility, does not indicate the depth of a relationship, and does not explain attraction.

---

[1] My books are available at :www.phoenixcentrepress.com

The. Best. Relationship. Ever.

Confusing sex with intimacy

In my book *This Endless Moment,* I wrote about a woman who broke off her engagement because she'd had sex (on a pool table!) with a friend. She talked about how hot and chargy it was.

I asked her why she'd broken off her engagement.

"I can't stay with my fiancé, because I must love [pool table guy] a lot! After all, I had great sex with him!"

I said, "Or you just got really horny, and had good sex. It was just sex."

She: "Oh no! I'd never have sex with someone just because he turns me on. I only have sex with people I love, and I must love him a lot, given how good the sex was."

Enough said? The problem is not having sex with a friend on a pool table. The problem comes from not being willing to admit that having sex is fun, in and of itself.

"I had sex with him/her, it must be love!" is idiocy. Unfortunately, it's really prevalent. And that's because we have such a hard time accepting ourselves as sexual beings.

It's so weird. People have such trouble saying. "I'm horny, and love to have sex!" This coyness around matters sexual originates in our fear of being "seen" as sexual. Most people are afraid to declare their sexual side, for fear of being judged as "perverse."

- True intimacy (being seen) *encompasses* sexuality, but is not equal to it.
- Sexuality is an intimate act – true intimacy is so much more.

Why You Fail at Relating

- True intimacy is the act of becoming open, honest, and vulnerable.
- True intimacy is the activity of sharing deeply and with verve.
- Most couples have sex, while never achieving true intimacy.

Because of our embarrassment over our sexual nature, we quickly mislabel sexual charge as 'love'

Sex is not equivalent to romance or love, and yet romance and love often contain, or provide a container for, our sexuality. Sexuality is a simple and very basic part of our being. It is what it is, and nothing more.

Take away point:

There is a real need for people to embrace their sexual nature. Far too often, people walk rapidly in the opposite direction. I am suggesting that we are all much better off identifying and accepting our nature as sexual beings, without making "a relationship" out of it.

There are an amazing number of relationships out there that exist only because the two people decided to bonk. They felt the sexual charge, and instead of swimming in the stream of sexuality, they made themselves guilty and decided they were "in love."

Or, conversely, some people dated, and discovered that they were sexually incompatible with their partner. Rather than moving on, the "...but we've had sex!!!" idiocy kicked in, and they moved into a relationship. They assumed that the sex would improve once they were "hooked up."

Yeah. Right. From that point on, their sexual life is a misery.

The. Best. Relationship. Ever.

We would like you to consider this: to see sex as sex, and to deal with it as such. This means that if you choose to be sexual only within a monogamous relationship, that's just great.

If you choose to enact your sexuality more broadly, this can be done through such things as erotic massage, sacred sexuality, "vulnerability projects," and the like, that's great too. (More on this in the Sexuality section.)

Sex is sex. We would be wise to celebrate it, and understand that it's much like other bodily functions – it's like digestion, like breathing. Taking our sexuality less seriously means that we can enjoy and appreciate the movement of energy in our bodies without making a song and dance out of it.

7. Betrayal

A betrayal happens when someone violates either our trust or our confidence. Betrayal causes us to tighten up and shut ourselves down, and this hurts physically. These physical sensations are real, and are an internal reaction that's triggered by how we choose to respond to the external betrayal.

Since we are conditioned to avoid pain, we often make the erroneous leap – If I never trust again, I will never be in pain again.

Unfortunately, (or fortunately...) pain in life is inevitable. People die. People leave us. Situations change, businesses and relationships fail. Natural and un-natural disasters happen. The resulting pain is one of the few certainties of life.

If you choose to be open, honest, and vulnerable, you *will* experience betrayal – someone will break your confidence, or violate your trust. It's not a matter of if, but when. And the

Why You Fail at Relating

closer the relationship between you and the other person, the more you will react to the betrayal. This is as it should be.

The wise soul expresses the pain, anger, sadness directly, loudly, and safely. You cry, you pound it out, you scream out your disappointment and sense of betrayal. You use your shut-down-ness to focus inward, to explore the pain, to own it, and to let it go. And then, you accept the reality of the betrayal, the authenticity of the pain, and you let it go. (See: "Ways to Express Emotions")

This is emphatically not what most people do. Instead of feeling and releasing the pain and the shut-down-ness, they adopt both as, "Who I am, from now on." Rather than process and work through the betrayal, they come up with two dumb ideas:

- I'll never be open, honest, and vulnerable again!
- I'll never form a deep and real relationship again! Better superficial than in pain!

Great, if your intention is to live a closed, dishonest, and blocked life. Not so great if you ever want to have **The. Best. Relationship. Ever.** – a relationship with depth, passion, purpose, and meaning.

There is almost a 100% certainty that you have been betrayed, in either a big way, or in a 100 little ways, and yet here you are, still alive. The betrayal(s) didn't kill you. They just hurt. Some might have hurt a lot. How *long* you choose to hold on to your hurt is up to you.

We're saying: "Allow yourself to hurt a lot and express it loudly...and then let it go."

Saying, "I'll never trust again!" means that you'll live in a self-created shell, as you anxiously wait for the next bad

The. Best. Relationship. Ever.

thing. Never trusting again is not an inoculation against pain – it's a prison sentence – it's solitary confinement.

The other option is to be real – to *accept* the reality of pain, death, sadness, abandonment, and betrayal – all of these things are part of you, part of being human.

No one 'likes' pain and hurt – by 'accept' I do not mean 'like.' By acceptance, I mean that you fully and completely understand that this is the nature of living – these things teach us to be resilient, alive, and compassionate.

The misguided thought, "If I avoid openness, honesty, and vulnerability, then nothing bad will happen, and I will never feel pain again," is nonsense. All it means is that future pain will come from isolation, uncertainty, distrust, and from shutting yourself down.

Being half (or less) of a person – out of fear, out of grief, out of uncertainty – means that you will never be known. Being known, being real, is all about feeling our feelings, thinking out thoughts, embracing our passions, enacting our sensuality and sexuality – and sharing 100% of ourselves.

No, not with everyone – the grocery clerk just wants your money, not your life story. But with a small and select group of intimates and primarily with your principal partner, open, honest, and vulnerable being must be the rule. No hiding, no evasions, no games.

To do this means confronting fear head on, accepting the universal nature of pain and loss, and choosing, again and again, to live fully and completely anyway.

Who you are becomes an open book, and those around you are seeing and interacting with the real you. And the real you is a process, not a fixed entity. You are evolving in your self-knowledge, and are evolving in your ability to remain open, honest, and vulnerable in the face of real living.

You recognize that some things you hear and see will lead you to want to shut down, to run, or to shift into doubt or confusion. You will share this openly with your partner, and will stay present while remaining open.

And because relating is a two-way street, you expect nothing less than real openness, total honesty, and complete vulnerability from your principal partner.

Being real is about being authentic and clear – not saying and doing things to fool your partner, or playing games to keep them around. Authenticity can be messy, but an inauthentic life stands out for its meaninglessness and lack of depth.

If you stay open, you'll discover that most things in life are fleeting and all of them can be worked through, shifted or accepted. Being real is the only option if you want your relationship to fly.

Take away point:

Open, honest, and vulnerable living entails the risk of betrayal. But so does all of living. Part of living is pain, sickness, death. With these things comes the possibility of disappointment, anger, or numbness.

No matter what we do, we have no choice but to feel. Refusing to be real, hiding your feelings, your thoughts, hopes and dreams from others, leads to the pain of isolation.

The key to fruitful living is accepting the reality of pain, while at the same time sharing, with your partner and with those you trust, who you are, what you are "made of" – sharing your fears, uncertainties, and doubts.

The. Best. Relationship. Ever.

The Communication Model you'll learn below will explain how to do this.

8. Playing games – Unspoken (Hidden) Intent

There are many types of hidden intent

Sexual Desire: I just flashed on the song, "All I want to do is make love to you," Sexual desire is a primary, often buried intent. It's clear, if we are honest with ourselves, that some or much of our behaviour with members of the gender we are attracted to has "being sexual with you" as an unspoken intent. Because it's not clearly expressed, it becomes an underlying tension.

Rage and revenge are often hidden intents. Many people want to get even when they hurt themselves over the behaviour of another. Rather than openly express the intent ("I'm really pissing myself off right now, and I'd love to dump you off a bridge,") they say something like "I just want you to be nicer," or "I just want you to acknowledge me as a person."

When I hear "just," I cringe. There's nothing 'just' about it. The dishonest expression of what's really going on means that nothing ever gets resolved.

Eternal Punishment: I ask clients to go deeper into their intent, and they often give me an endless list of their partner's sins – years' worth of stuff. I'll hear, "When my partner makes amends for all of this, then I'll consider letting up. Until then, I'll just keep complaining and demanding." This hidden intent doesn't match at all with "I just want him to talk to me more." It does match with, "I haven't extracted my pound of flesh yet."

Why You Fail at Relating

Shallowly Expressed Intents

- "I just wish my husband was strong and independent," masks, "I want him to always come home and ask me what to do, so I can tell him."
- "I just want a better relationship," masks, "I'm going to make him behave by turning him into the man he ought to be, or else."
- "I just tell her things for her own good," masks, "She should know that I have all the answers about how this relationship should be. She'd be so much happier doing it my way."
- "You never listen to me" masks, "You never do what I tell you."
- "You're always looking at other (wo)men" masks, "I'm really insecure about my self-image and our relationship."

Take away:

Once we openly and honestly begin to explore and share our intentions, we can see how ridiculous, manipulative, and destructive many of the hidden ones are.

We can then begin to surface intentions that are simple and direct

- "My intent is to deepen my relationship with you by being open and honest and vulnerable."
- "My intent is to own and express my attempts to manipulate you."
- "My intent is to treat you as an equal adult, not as a/an (object, sex object, kid, enemy, etc.)"

Failing at Communication

No question: I'm an elegant communication junkie. I think communication is so important that I've created this

The. Best. Relationship. Ever.

separate 'bad' communication section. I am convinced that 'bad' communication is the issue most likely to destroy relationships.

I'm going to be talking about using a Communication Model later on in the book, so I'll limit myself here to mentioning a few ways people pretend to communicate – ways that create issues, confusion, and a lessening of open, honest, and vulnerable relating. I'll also briefly present some suggestions for doing communication differently.

Problem: About vs. At

This is shorthand for how one "aims" one's words. The Communication Model stresses "I" language vs. "you" language, and this parallels "about" and "at." "I" language is "about how I am doing" language, and "you" language is "aimed at blaming you" language.

"At" language is the language of attack and blame

It's directed "at" your partner, using a critical tone of voice – yelling, frustration, and long, boring lectures.

It sounds like:

"You disappoint me. You need to listen, to communicate my way, to live in the house the way I want you to, and to do what I want you to. Is that so hard?"

The recipient of this "at" attack typically either fights back, or acquiesces, only to return to the criticized behaviour as soon as the lecturer's back is turned.

"About" language, on the other hand, is me, speaking from where "I" am

The language of elegant communication is personal. "I am feeling, I am thinking, I observe, I intend..." and then, what I do. It acknowledges our 100% principle: what is happening for me is all about me – therefore blaming others is wrong-headed and silly. (See: "Speaking Clearly...")

Let's be clear here: Learning to communicate well takes constant effort and vigilance

Darbella and I, even after decades of communicating well, still notice a pull to criticize and defend. Even with very precise language, our Egos lurk in the background, seeking evidence that we are "being hard-done by." The little voice inside starts shouting: "Yeah, but you do it too! And besides, you're more screwed up than I am!" strangeness.

- This book is not about trying to eliminate such *thoughts* – that's impossible.
- What you must do is stop saying dumb things – stop *verbally* "at-ing."

What I think never gets me in trouble. How I say what I am thinking, on the other hand, can be deadly. We therefore use the Communication Model to express all of our thoughts responsibly

Problem: Protected vs. Open

A simple way to explore your protection techniques is to ask yourself, "What do I *resist* talking about?"

Now, you may want to change the word "resist" to "dodge," or "divert myself from," or "only speak half-truths about," but you get the idea.

Protecting yourself from your fear of dire outcomes means you'll always be hiding. Many times I've seen people

The. Best. Relationship. Ever.

tuck their thoughts, desires, and feelings away, not wanting a confrontation. They hide and hide, and then something happens, and the relationship is over. And then all of the blocked material flows out, after it's too late.

Now, the usual caveats apply. There are degrees of openness, meaning that we do not owe total revelation to the grocery clerk. We do, however, hide things from our principal partner at our peril.

Openness is revealing what you know about yourself

It's not about the other person. I can only be open about me. So, with Darbella, I might say, "Here is what I am going to do, and here is the process I took to get there." I'm doing the latter because she is interested in my thinking process, (and I am interested in hers.)

I am not telling her stuff to gain permission or approval, as she can offer me neither

With others, "Here is how it is for me" is often sufficient. In order to do this successfully, you need to let go of biting on the drama others create, and clearly (and perhaps repeatedly) state who and where you are.

Openness is letting the people you care about know who you are, and where you are. It's one of the most important aspects of relating with elegance. This also means, in an EIR, the listener chooses to listen openly, without "biting," while remaining curious about the speaker.

Problem: Sensitivity vs. Insensitivity

People in less than functional relationships seem to be "signal insensitive." Let me give you an example.

Why You Fail at Relating

A couple comes in. They've been married for 40 years. I observe the following:

- When they talk with each other, they do not make eye contact.
- They talk "at," not "about."
- The tone of voice is what I'd call "the exasperated lecture."
- They tell each other that, "You're totally wrong, you don't get it," and then present examples that are 35 years old.
- Both sit in a posture of defensive aggression, leaning slightly forward, while pointing their index fingers at each other.

I could go on, but I trust you have a picture in mind.

Each person's intent is to "win" – it is emphatically not to share, to listen, or to be curious. Each has a perspective on what "ought to be done," and both have been doing the same things for 40 years. Never, once, has what they are doing achieved what they say they want.

So, they do the same thing harder, longer.

I call this Signal Insensitive

Let's take things at face value and assume that this couple wants to communicate. If they were paying attention, they'd see clearly that their choice of action isn't working.

They'd *also* see their partner leaning away, shutting down, looking the other way, crossing their arms, behaving defensively.

The signals are right there, and they miss them. Or ignore them. Or devalue them. Too busy, I think, trying to "win and be right."

The. Best. Relationship. Ever.

Elegant Communication Means Paying Attention

It's not enough to learn a Communication Model if all you are going to do is try it once, then shut down and not notice what happens next.

To use "loudness" as an example, people who deliver their "stuff" with volume and verve will claim, "That's just how I am!" No matter that their partner, on the receiving end, is pressed up against the wall, twitching. The loudness actually covers over a deep insecurity over appearing open and vulnerable, although on the surface it appears as bravado.

What is significant, however, is what is actually happening

Following along with the example regarding the couple above: when I suggested that both change their approach, they immediately crossed their arms across their chests, smirked a bit, and subtly shook their heads, "No."

I noticed, stopped mid-sentence, and said, "So, I notice that as I suggest changes, both of you cross your arms and shake your heads, "No." I'm wondering if you have come here to see if I can make work what doesn't work, or whether you're willing to change what you are doing."

Both made it clear that I didn't understand, and that change was the last thing they were looking for.

Now, had I not noticed and shifted my tack, I'd have been sitting there frustrating myself, while they tuned me out. Not productive. Since I did notice, I could shift from the theoretical (things they could try at home) to the 'real' – what was going on, right there, right now.

Time for a case study that describes how "going off the rails" works. After that, we'll begin the process of creating **The. Best. Relationship. Ever.**

Chapter Two: A case study in weird relating

The Ballad of Sally and Sam

Let's follow Sam and Sally through the course of their relationship, both prior to, and during therapy. As we go along, I will give you more and more information about them, so you can see how this works.

Sam and Sally are not new to the dating game. Both have seen relationships come and go, and both are cautious. When they met, their minimum requirements for 'acceptable dating material' were fulfilled. Sam and Sally start dating.

This is the **Friendship** stage. Sam and Sally, because of past failures in relating, remain cautious, yet optimistic. They both see 'potential' in the other – traits such as loyalty, steadfastness, and fascination with each other are obvious in their early dates.

So, of course, is an underlying tingle – the hormonal charge of lust. They remember past experiences of moving too fast, so they decide to hold off on intercourse… and spend time on "the other bases."

They spend a month or so at the **Friendship** stage, and "all systems are go" – no red flags, lots of fun dates, they feel close and warm toward each other, and also seem to be communicating with openness. However, they are operating out of habit, and are not aware of their **dating behaviour**.

Dating Behaviour: Both realize that there are aspects of their personality and history that their new partner will find weird, difficult, or just plain strange. Not wanting the object of their lust and interest to run away, they do not trot out the whole package – they trot out only the parts that they think will get their partner to stick around.

In the advertising biz, this is called, "selling the sizzle."

The combination of not being honest and the blindness that lust produces is missed by both of them.

After a month two, they stumble into the **Friends with Benefits (FWB)** stage

Sexual Patterning

As soon as their relationship moves past casual dating, another, incredibly powerful paradigm emerges. The paradigm is, "My sexual patterning."

This patterning has two levels:

Biological – we cannot escape our genetics. Humans are hormonally designed to mate, breed, and propagate their DNA. There has been a ton of research on this – how "cues" exist, for both sexes, which operate under the level of awareness. Scent, body shape, eye-contact, and other physical attributes trigger the release of pleasure hormones. These signals, if we continue to "not notice," drive us to turn a blind eye to other signals.

Historical – here's where our back story gets added in. Our sexual experiences (or lack of them) colour how we 'see'

The. Best. Relationship. Ever.

and respond to what is going on sexually with our partner. If there has been any "weirdness" in a back story, (abuse, lack of affection and touching, hyper-sexualized family members, or a hyper-sexualized personal history, etc.) this highly relevant story might be pushed into the background by hormones / lust. But history will re-emerge.

Sally's sexual history played a big part in what happened next. The fact that she'd refrained from having sex with Sam was quite amazing. Sally loved sex.

Sally was therefore ecstatic when they were ready for the **FWB** stage. She later realized that she was the initiator almost all of the time, although Sam seemed enthusiastic.

For a while, having sex covered over increasing tensions over expectations re. communication, their careers, how they related with others – the veneer was slipping a bit.

Sam wasn't as communicative, and really seemed to like watching his new TV. Sally was locked in to buying sexy outfits, and playing seduction games. There were moments of bickering, usually paved over with cuddling, "sweet talk," and sex.

Several months in, the first signs of a "disconnect" appeared. Both were still in lust, so there was a ton of denial. Sally and Sam were looking at each other with less starry eyes. There were spending more time apart, and the sex was losing its charge.

Despite warning signs, Sam says, "Wow! 6 months! I'm so happy. Let's get married!"

Here comes the Committed Relationship stage

In retrospect, neither could remember why they agreed to get married. Sam mentioned it, and it seemed reasonable.

Why You Fail at Relating

After all, they did have 6 months in... and they were having sex, and friends and family were urging them to "get serious."

They were totally missing the warning signals of "unprocessed stuff, arising from the depths." Dumb relationships are like rolling a snowball down a hill – it soon gets huge, and takes on a momentum of its own.

Also forgotten in the rush was past experience – other failed relationships had started the same way. Plus, Sam thought, Sally looked really, really good in those sexy outfits...

So, they got engaged, and then got married.

The Triggering Event

For Sam and Sally, the distracting "joy of marriage" continued for six months or so. 'Bad' behaviours were ignored, despite that niggling little voice, "I hate that about Sally, but she loves me, so I'll cut her some slack." No matter who Sally actually was, Sam compared her to his internal "imaginary friend" – and struggled to fit Sally to this pattern – subconsciously, of course.

And Sally was doing the same with Sam

(Let me note that "marriage" is not required for this to happen. Every relationship reaches this point. Creating the drama and distraction of engagement and marriage often just delays the inevitable. With an open and honest relationship right from the start, this bump is dramatically minimized.)

No telling in advance what the triggering event will be, but it happens to everyone

Sam woke up one morning, and finally saw (stopped disregarding) behaviour from Sally that he really, really hated.

The. Best. Relationship. Ever.

Fear niggled at Sam's brain stem, and a cold sweat started to form. He quickly got himself under control, and attempted to blow the fear off. No dice.

According to Sam, Sally was clearly and plainly *wrong*.

Sam's triggering event: Sam watched Sally get ready for work, and, for the first time, *really noticed* she was dressed in a mini miniskirt. Sam dredged up an old belief: *wives* are not supposed to be 'sexy.'

In rapid succession, Sam decided: Sally should be demure, dress 'appropriately,' (the way Sam wanted her to,) should turn to him for advice about everything, and should stay home, and be a 'satisfied wife.'

Sally was confused, and refused outright, and loudly, to be dictated to. Sally was chagrined that Sam was acting "just like her dad," who had been endlessly critical. Sally had a career, always wore mini-skirts and high heels, and loved turning heads.

Sally dug in her heels (so to speak,) and spoke to Sam like she'd spoken to her dad when she was 16 – right before she moved out for good. Sally was belligerent, sarcastic, and angry.

Sam couldn't figure out why Sally no longer 'fit.' Sam tried to fix her. Then he started to blame Sally for deceiving him, for refusing to change to make him happy.

Then he noticed other hateful behaviours

One day, Sam, holus bolus, switched from "Sally, my perfect partner" to "Sally, the devil's spawn." This became his new belief, and was tied to another old story of his – "You can't trust women."

From that point on, all Sam saw were the behaviours he hated

Why? In the early going, both Sam and Sally were wearing "rose coloured sunglasses." They only saw behaviours that made it through the "lust / love / breeding, minimum requirements" filters. Everything appeared to be perfect – everything was "rosy."

With time, the fantasy fades and the real person emerges. It's a short stroll to, "I've been betrayed now, as I was betrayed before – I can't trust anyone."

Sam removed his rose coloured glasses and put on the blue pair. Now, everything is seen through the new, "devil's spawn" belief. It doesn't matter that Sally's 'hateful' behaviour happens 1 in a 100 times. Sam can say with a straight face, "She lied to me about everything! Now I know the truth."

Well, no she didn't – and no he doesn't.

All Sam has is new information, and he doesn't know what to do with it.

How we shift from one story to another, and why each story seems 'true'

Sam's shifting from Sally = perfect to Sally = the devil's spawn, from a neurological perspective, is nothing more than a database search that leads, through repetition, to a synaptic rewire job.

How this works: On my computer, I can set up an enquiry in any database I have. Say I search my mailing list for "Canada." The database spits out everyone from Canada and no one from anywhere else (assuming that my data was put in correctly in the first place! Remember this!)

The. Best. Relationship. Ever.

If I tell my brain to sort my "Sally" database, and I set the search parameter as "Sally = the devil's spawn," *that's all I will get*. The system does not correct my search. It gives me what I ask for, in spades.

In the prior relational stages, Sam was focused on (searching for) "Sally = my perfect partner." However, *all* the other stuff was being stored too – the things Sam was not noticing. Because this data did not match what Sam was looking for, the 'negative' data never reached Sam's awareness.

I also have a database called "Sally."

It consists of her in counselling sessions, plus other interactions with Sally as a child, pre-teen, and teen. I have a few from her early adult time, and from when she and Sam were clients. Because I am not Sally's spouse, my database is fairly neutral.

Now, this should be obvious: my database in no way matches Sam's. I saw (and filtered) what I saw, and so did Sam. In neither case is our internal database about "Sally." It's about my version and Sam's version of Sally. It's me, my data, and I'm in my head, in a sense, acting out the Wayne version of Sally.

Sam eventually learned to let go of viewing Sally according to sequential rigid stages – friend, FWB, etc. He learned to do a 'brain-dump query.'

It is this: "Give me *all* data concerning Sally." This will produce the totality of his stored data experience of Sally, devoid of judgement. (The judgement is Sally = the devil's spawn.)

Elegant relating requires that Sam be present with Sally – the total person – not just the parts that agree with his pre-judgements. Elegant relating is the process of adding this moment to the pre-existing data – here is what I know (have in my brain) regarding Sally, and I add my present experience to it.

I suggested to Sally and Sam a better way of relating

It is a more productive, inclusive approach, which seeks to accept the whole of what is – not just the acceptable, the fun, the culturally acceptable parts, but all of it. And of course the joke is, we are whole (and part of our wholeness is all of the weird stuff, as well as the chargy bits...), whether we want to be or not. We are as we are, no matter how much we wish it was otherwise. And so is our partner.

A metaphor for escaping the drama – creating flexible containers

A flexible container accepts and holds whatever is put in. As we add understandings to it, it expands and conforms in shape to the new information – and is thus capable of holding infinitely expanding content.

If, instead of shifting to, "Sally, the bad person," I have a container called "Sally, as she is," it should be obvious this container can hold the whole package of my understanding of Sally – 'good, bad, and indifferent' – and that I can add new information at will, as it becomes available to me.

If Sam chose to do this, he would be aware of the Sally he was interacting with, not the distorted, limited version.

He then could make a clean decision about being with her, or not, based on his perception of everything he knows about Sally, not just the part that matches some artificial, preconceived idea of how "a wife" should be.

The. Best. Relationship. Ever.

Flexible containerizing is an action – a way of relating

If I am wise, I realize that people are as they are – not what they tell us, not how I judge them, not how I imagine or wish them to be, but rather how they actually live their lives – and who they are is a dynamic process.

If Sally and Sam do not come to understand this, their relationship will be a misery. They will waste inordinate amounts of time trying to get the other to behave – to do things the 'right' way. There will be moments of détente – tenuous peace, followed by ever increasing levels of anger, resentment, blame and sadness.

Elegant relating has no judgement connected to it

Elegant relating is choosing to see and accept all of my data. Sam, for example, sees Sally as she is, and drops his Ego-driven need to force her to be other than she is.

As Sam makes the moment-by-moment decision to 'wake up' and be present with the real Sally, the next question is, "Given all of this data, including the present chunk, how do I wish to engage with Sally in this moment?"

This, for most, is way, way too simple

Most of us are invested in the work we have done with the data in our heads. In fact, we have spent most of our lives being non-present, up in our heads, like mad librarians, cataloguing and analyzing the experiences stored there. We are so nuts that we think that the card catalogue of past events is more important and relevant than what we are actually experiencing in the moment.

The bottom line here is that we have learned to do this categorizing thing, and we use it as a mask to keep ourselves hidden. In doing so, we know less about the other person, because the mask filters our curiosity. Once we throw away the mask, especially in our relationship, we are both present and available for intimacy.

OK, let's shift gears, and look at how Elegant, Intimate Relating works

And also, a bit more from Sally and Sam!

Chapter Three: A New Model for Relating

In order to have **The. Best. Relationship. Ever.,** you must change your way of relating. This requires rigorous self-exploration, and openness, honesty, and curiosity.

Mostly, because we're lazy, we tend to repeat what doesn't work. Or, we try out a technique for a bit, and when there's a bump in the road, we pull out old, non-functional ways of relating.

We get stuck in a rut, and blame the rut

Failed relating follows a pattern – the same one Sam and Sally followed. There are not many variations on this theme – get into a primary relationship at a young age, flounder about, get lousy results, end the relationship... and then... do it again!

We do this in other areas of our lives as well – for example, in academic fields we don't like. We don't take the time to learn a new way – we just repeat what doesn't work, and whine about our lousy results.

Here's an example: I'm not so good at algebra. I got through it in High School and University, but never really figured it out. I did enough to pass. I memorized a few patterns, and studied old tests, and learned what I call "brute force" algebra. I have a few rules in my head, but absolutely no understanding.

Because I like to torture myself, when Darbella (who is great at math) taught algebra to her 8th grade Math students, I'd occasionally try one of the more complicated problems.

I'd just loop endlessly, trying to "simplify the equation." Then I'd spend a bit of time moving things from one side of the = sign to the other.

I did what I always do with algebra problems. I guess, I try a few things I've tried before, and I hope that I will luck into an answer. Believe me, it is not a pretty sight.

Dar, on the other hand, just looks at the problem, applies logical and elegant steps, and solves it quickly. She can do this (and make it look simple!) because she 'gets' what underlies algebra.

Here's how this applies to relationships

I don't 'get' algebra, *and* I am unwilling to expend the effort to learn.

This is how most people deal with relating. They learn a few 'rules' in adolescence, typically from other ignorant people. Once they establish a pattern of behaviour, they apply the techniques out of blind habit and Ego, and think that, this time, they'll get the 'right' answer.

They lack understanding, and may even be unaware how little they know about relating

Now, sometimes, rarely, this "brute force, unconscious" approach does work, giving one false hope. As I said, I passed

The. Best. Relationship. Ever.

algebra. I just never got good at it, or understood it. For me, to this day, algebra is a misery.

Acting from "unawareness" is limiting, disrespectful and leads back to the "I'm right and you need to see things my way."

It's a rule: if all I do is what I always do, plus cross my fingers, mostly, all I'll get is lousy results. If I want to succeed, I must first deeply understand, and then apply, elegant solutions.

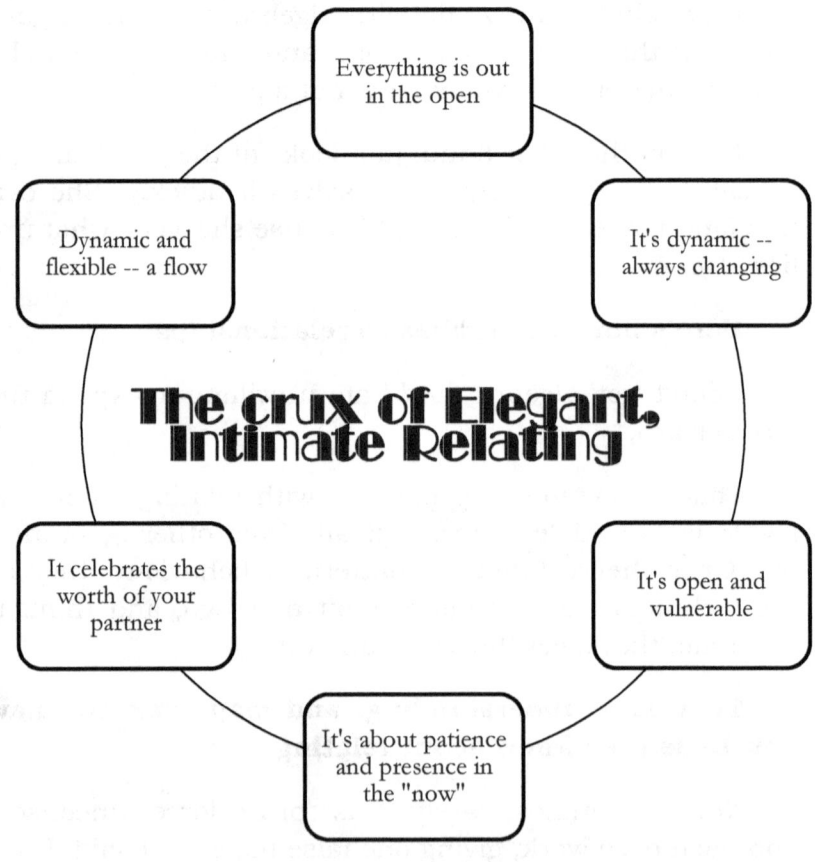

- **The elegant part is this:** an elegant relationship is both dynamic and flexible. There's a flow – an ease. While there are different roles to explore, nothing is rigid, and everything is available.
- **The intimate part is this**: everything is out in the open, revealed, and honestly discussed. It is all about truthfulness, a relaxation of boundaries, and clear focus.
- **Elegant, Intimate Relating is dynamic**: while the methodology of relating stays the same, there is *acceptance* that "life" is constantly in flux. Emotions arise, and shift, and change. Roles shift, depending on the needs and desires of the partners. Nothing is graven in stone.
- **Both partners are open and vulnerable**: everything is accepted as real, and all feelings are fully felt and shared, without judgement, without trying to get your partner to behave some other way.
- **Elegant, Intimate Relating is Respectful:** it's recognizing and celebrating the worth of your partner. It is impossible to respect someone for what he or she is *going to* do or be, someday, if all is well and "the creek don't rise." Respect is acknowledging the *present* worth of another person. Therefore, I can only "recognize and celebrate" someone right now.
- **Elegant, Intimate Relating Requires Patience:** it's knowing that all I can do right now is what I can do *right now*. Patience is the ability to be present with things, situations, and people – while fully grasping that everyone and everything is in flux. "Things are as they are, until they aren't."

Everything is complete at every stage, while at the same time is moving with time toward a state of 'more complete.' This is a difficult concept.

The. Best. Relationship. Ever.

Think about building a bridge. At every stage, each step – say, setting the pylons into the river – is 'complete' as it progresses. When they are digging the hole, that's it – they are digging. Then, mixing concrete. Then, pouring concrete. Each step is, in its moment, a whole. In terms of each step's 'bridge-ness,' it is *also* part of that process.

Thus, how it is *right now* is what to focus on – not how you wish it was, nor about how it used to be. Elegant, Intimate Relating is about living fully in the present moment.

Elegant, Intimate Relating is All about Intent

Elegant relating requires finding new ways of seeing and processing what is happening.

This is best accomplished by having a clue as to what I am trying to accomplish (my Intent,) all the time. Otherwise I will find that I am going off half-cocked.

So, if my goal is to relate with honesty and intimacy, any behaviour that does not facilitate this goal must be stopped as it emerges.

Example: Absolutist phrasing ("You are [always, never, every time, right wrong, etc.] doing...") leads to fighting about whether the absolute is 'true.' It's also limiting, disrespectful, and leads back to "I'm right and you need to see things my way."

Once I know this, I can stop myself from making absolute statements, and say instead, "I'm noticing [whatever] and I wonder what's going on for you."

Good communicators will ask their partner, "What was your intent in asking me that?" It's also a legitimate question for you to ask yourself. Just don't stop too soon. Because intent is often not what you first think it is.

● ● ●

Intent has to be expressed with total honesty. Hiding your intentions leads down a path we'd best avoid.

We'll be fleshing out these concepts in the Tools Section, but I trust you're getting an inkling about how different **The. Best. Relationship. Ever.** is from a 'normal' relationship. We're going to continue to flesh out the concepts – next up – let's talk about Dialogue.

The key to elegant relating is dialogue

Ongoing dialogue is a hard choice, and is selected by perhaps 5% of couples. Open, honest, vulnerable dialogue leads to a sense of aliveness, vibration and vibrancy, and energized living. Its characteristics are curiosity, passion, integrity, and co-creativity.

Wise souls take conflict personally

In other words, they examine themselves – to their personal participation – rather than placing blame. The wise soul looks at his behaviour – whatever isn't working – and chooses to do something different.

Letting go of the need to be right is a vital part of elegant living, and essential for Elegant, Intimate Relating.

Understanding that differences are differences of *opinion*, not fact, is the mark of the beginning of maturity. Letting go of the need to be right allows me to become curious about who my partner is, and how he / she operates – differently than I do, yet never wrong.

A bit about fighting

"I never want to fight with my partner again!" is unreasonable. A fight, in a sense, is ending up on the other side of

The. Best. Relationship. Ever.

an issue you and your partner are passionate about. Passion is good!

Things go off the rails when either or both parties are neither aware nor present.

Here's the story of all 'bad' fights

Person A notices something. It could be a "thing," or behaviour. Let's say it's an unwashed coffee cup.

The coffee cup has no meaning – it's neutral.

1st fork in the road:

Person A could say, "There's an unwashed coffee cup. I'll wash it." No fight.

Or, Person A could say, "Geez, you forgot to wash the cup! You're a lousy housekeeper, and besides, you do that to annoy me!" Hand grenade.

The first response is "what I am noticing." The second response is: "I have a belief that my partner disrespects me, and this is another example."

Person B now has the ball.

Person B might bite. "Up yours. I'm not the only one around here with hands, you know. Besides, I pick up for you all the time, and don't bitch about it. I'm sick of your attitude." Person B lobs the hand grenade back.

Or, Person B could say, "I notice you seem to be upsetting yourself, and I'm curious as to your intention." Attempt to neutralize, and enter dialogue.

There is always a choice!

A New Model for Relating

The rest of this book is about learning to pay attention to our process, how we upset ourselves, and how we talk. Fights start because both parties get caught up in proving the other person is either wrong, an ass, or both. Fights are short-circuited when one of the parties chooses to stop the drama, and becomes curious.

This is done through dialogue

We're alive, I believe, to learn who we are – to expand and deepen our self-knowledge. We must do this in dialogue, because we are so good at self-justification – otherwise known as lying to ourselves. Without dialogue, we continue to make our crappy lives a misery – all the while focussing on what the other person (or the situation) is 'doing' to us.

Elegant Dialogue has several characteristics

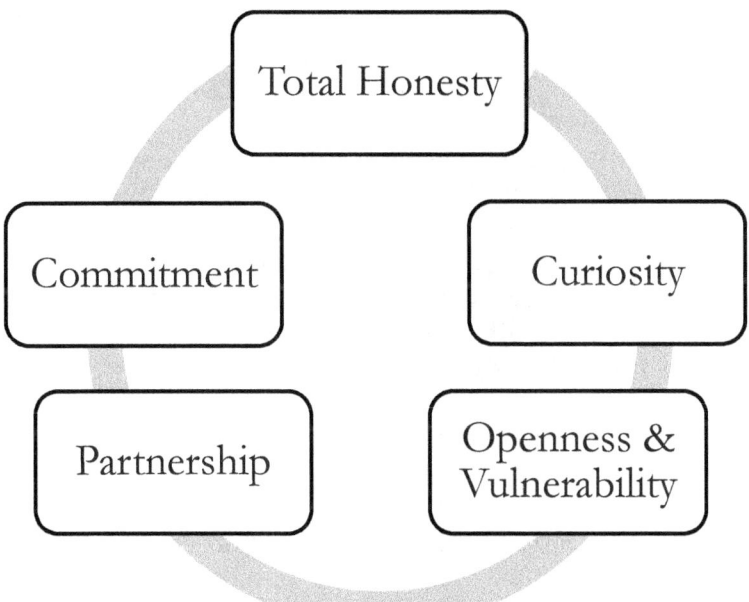

The. Best. Relationship. Ever.

- **The chief characteristic is *total honesty*.** This means that you keep your partner "in the loop" – you tell your partner what's up for you – and you do this all the time. There are no secrets, no games, no lying.
- **The second characteristic is *curiosity*.** This is deep interest in your partner's growth and 'truth.' Curiosity requires giving up a great illusion – that you know anything at all about your partner's experience. Once you realize that you barely know yourself, let alone know your partner's intention, thoughts, and desires, you can let go of erroneous mind-reading, and *ask*.
- **The third characteristic is *openness and vulnerability*.** *Openness* is the willingness to drop your guardedness so that you hear your partner's experience. When working with clients, I encourage them to "show openness" by uncrossing their arms, resting them on the armrests, and sitting with their legs uncrossed, and knees slightly apart. As mammals, we are "belly shy," so being unguarded in this way signals trust.
- **Openness is about *inviting dialogue*.** This is shown through language such as, "Tell me more," "Keep going," "I'm curious about you," etc. In Star Trek terminology, it's "Shields Down!"
- ***Vulnerability* is the other side of the coin.** Being vulnerable means, "I choose to reveal everything, including information that is difficult for me to speak." No excuses, no delay, no looking for the 'right time.' Vulnerability differs from honesty, which is telling the truth about everything – vulnerability means going even deeper – choosing to risk fully sharing your defended, scary, evil, or weird 'stuff.'
- **The fourth characteristic is *partnership*.** Couples see themselves as "in this together," much like partners in a business. Couples take each other's side in all external conflict – they never take the side of an outsider. Partners look for solutions – for ways to resolve issues, and to do so quickly and elegantly.

• • •

- **The fifth characteristic is *commitment*.** In successful relationships, people do not commit to each other. They commit to a way of being and relating.

Integrity holds it all together

Integrity means doing what you say you'll do. Integrity means that my words and actions match. Integrity is never dependent upon the behaviour of others. Integrity is a personal characteristic or attribute – and is solely demonstrated by how and whether I live up to what I have committed to.

I can only commit to an action – to something I will do

Think about it. You cannot commit to a person or cause. You can only commit to your behaviour toward a person or cause.

Many are unwilling to make anything other than conditional commitments. "I'll do this if you do that, and you get to go first, of course." It's a variation on an old theme – "If you love me, you'll behave the way I want you to, so that I don't have any conflicts, or work to do." Any such statement demonstrates a complete lack of integrity.

Integrity between partners plays out in mutual respect and honesty, integrity and forthrightness. No games, no manipulation, no trying to force the other person into a "shape" of your making.

The Core of Elegant, Intimate Relating

As Sam and Sally spoke with each other in my office, I helped them to learn how to be open, honest, and vulnerable. I showed them how to sit, how to uncross their limbs, and how to speak using "I" language.

The. Best. Relationship. Ever.

Like most, Sally and Sam had resisted deep self-revelation

Why? It's pretty simple. We hate many aspects of ourselves. We feel our emotions directly, and as they rattle our insides, we hurt. We watch the movies we create in our heads, and thank 'god' no one else can see the things we say and do in there. We are sure that if our partner ever watched our internal movies, they'd run for the door.

And we assume that we are the only one doing this, the only one who is this 'bad, evil, and perverted,' whatever. We're ashamed of ourselves, and scared the secret will get out.

Then, our partner inadvertently lets one of their cats out of the bag, and we pounce. "You lied to me!" We conveniently forget all of the crap we are stuffing, and turn the whole thing inside out, blaming 'the other' our partner has become.

Sam and Sally had been playing this dysfunctional game for several months.

I helped them to embrace an alternative, which is as simple as, "If I have nothing to hide, there is nothing hidden." This is about one's willingness to open up and say what's going on, because that's the only way to get anywhere. In this process of saying, of revealing, one learns to respect, forgive, and (horrors!) even love oneself.

Curiosity and Acceptance

Curiosity is an interesting thing. Often, poorly trained communicators think curiosity means that others should be endlessly curious about them – about every detail of their life. This becomes their focus, and it is never reciprocal.

A New Model for Relating

Actually, this is 180 degrees off.

Curiosity is my internal process, as I interact with others.

- I listen, and ask for clarification if I'm confusing myself. I say, "I'm curious as to what you intend by your words or actions."
- I compare the experience I am presently having with my past experiences with my partner, and add new information to my description of my partner.
- I hear what my partner is saying, see what my partner is doing, and if the two do not 'match,' I ask for more information.

Acceptance: Acceptance is choosing to relate to the totality of my partner – to a "whole person." I am not relating to the parts I like while rejecting the rest. I continually work toward a more complete internal picture of the other person. To do so, I must add and incorporate new data. That I might not 'like' certain of my partner's characteristics is about me, not about my partner.

The opposite of acceptance is judgement

I can never figure out why people endlessly criticize and blame their partners, or put their partners down. I don't 'get' people who mock or berate their partners, either to their face, or to others. I do not understand why one would do that to the person they are choosing to spend their life with. Nor do I understand why anyone thinks they have the right to do this.

Yet, blame and criticism (judgement) seem to infect most relationships.

The. Best. Relationship. Ever.

Here are two truths:

First, your partner is exactly and precisely how they act. Given how he or she acts, the only two viable choices regarding your relationship are:

- Total acceptance, or
- Packing your bag and leaving.
- The third option, endless carping, manipulating, fighting, judging, is just stupid.

Second, you are not there to fix your partner. You can only fix yourself. Your job is to work on yourself, and to share yourself with your partner. And your partner, in a healthy relationship, does the same. Each step along the way, my task is to integrate my 'new partner' (today's new data) into my present picture or file. Nothing more, nothing less.

Self-Responsible Relating

In the next few sections, we'll explore precise methods for communicating, for bring open, honest, and vulnerable, and for creating specific Vulnerability Projects designed to help you to explore hidden, or scary, or chargy aspects of your Self.

Chapter Four: Tools for Relating

Elegant, Intimate Relating (EIR)

EIR is a structure for living deeply and fully with others

With EIR, nothing is taken for granted. Elegant, Intimate Relating requires the active participation of two separate and distinct beings, both of whom are dedicated to rigorous self-exploration. Each is using the relationship to gain depth and breadth of knowledge about the only thing each can know: themselves.

Elegant, Intimate Relating is enacted at the direct meeting of two whole persons. I call this "meeting at the boundary" – I am still I, you are still you, and we meet to explore, to reveal, to be open and vulnerable through honest revelation.

The revelation has to be authentic

In EIR, you are choosing to be transparent with your partner. EIR is not about saying nice things, not about manipulating your partner to see or do things your way. Nor is it about hiding the fact that you have a range of feelings and emotions "in there." Transparent authenticity is choosing to let yourself be seen – as you are, and how you are.

The. Best. Relationship. Ever.

Elegant, Intimate Relating happens only in the Here and Now

It's about true vulnerability. Vulnerability happens as I choose to reveal my internal experience and intentions, as opposed to using them as a basis for manipulation.

Vulnerability is expressed by letting out what is going on for you, right now, with no excuses. This is me, right now. And part of "me, right now," is the emotion that is happening inside of me. Not descriptions of the emotions, not blaming someone for the emotions, but rather the emotions themselves.

Once you "get this," you'll also notice that emotions are fleeting. I can be sad, then bored, then weepy, then laugh-filled, then have the feeling of "nothing much," but only if *I do not cling to* my story, a.k.a. thinking too much.

Being unguarded

Un-guarding yourself means being willing to own and share your in-the-moment reality, without filtering. Being unguarded means speaking your truth – the truth that comes from "Here is what is so for me..."

The point of Elegant, Intimate Relating is to clear the decks so that you can shift what is not working. Letting go of guardedness gives us the opportunity to see how we are structuring our stories to stay stuck. From there, you choose to do something new and refreshing. It's not meant as an exercise in self-aggrandizement, and emphatically is not a game to stay stuck, while *pretending* to "get it."

Un-guarding means loosening the filters, and expressing yourself as you are, with focus and clarity.

The Beginning of Elegant, Intimate Relating

The Tools section of the book describes the "how" of an EIR. Here's the "what."

Engaged Intimacy, first of all, requires a dialogue agreement

Let me whip out my crystal ball and declare that your past relationship failures were caused by poor, faulty, or non-existent verbal communication. Other problems were: non-verbal communication, magical thinking, lack of physical intimacy, and lack of self-responsibility.

We are going to establish a dialogue agreement, and then discuss how to enact it.

The Dialogue Agreement

"I have decided to commit myself to open, honest, and vulnerable communication. I will use a Communication Model, self-responsible language, and will keep my boundaries open and flexible. I will be in dialogue with you for no less than 30 minutes per day, and when issues cannot be resolved within that time-frame, I agree to make as much time as necessary to resolve the issue, with no compromise. I commit to keep you totally informed about what is going on for me: my stories, my games, my evasions. I will keep you completely informed about my feelings, my attractions, and my other relationships. I do so not for permission, but to facilitate clarity."

The Physical Contact Agreement

Given that we're discussing your Primary Relationship, physical contact is a given. We've noted that Engaged Intimacy is also available for other relationships. I think it's important to establish physical parameters, even within the Primary Relationship. Thus:

The. Best. Relationship. Ever.

"I commit to using physical contact as another way of exploring my emotions, blockages, and my connection with you. I accept that physical contact is an end unto itself – that it is not primarily a means to having sex. I will be open and honest about my need for emotional expression, and will use safe methods of expressing my emotions thoroughly. I will ask for what I want as regards physical contact, recognizing that what I want "now," may not be what I want "later." I am open to expressing whatever feelings arise through physical contact, will stay focussed on myself, and will feel my feelings fully."

This becomes the framework for Engaged Intimacy

From this baseline, which you are free to add to, but not reduce, we begin the process of building intimacy and presence. I would suggest that you look carefully at the above Agreements, and then read through the "Tools" chapters to follow. Once you have a grasp on how this all fits together, sit with your partner, begin right here with the Agreements, and structure your own agreements.

You will want to write out what you are agreeing to, and then sign it. Remember: all you can agree to is what *you* will do. This is not a conditional, "If you do this, then I'll do that" kind of agreement. You are making the commitment to yourself to act in a certain way, while in your partner's presence. I'll be reminding you of that as we go along.

The 9 Tools

The Structure

It is our belief that self-knowing happens best in your Primary Relationship. This relationship has as its keys: elegant communication, vulnerability, (the willingness to open up) openness, (the willingness to take in) and intimacy (making full, honest contact.)

Through dialogue, baseline parameters are set, in the following two areas:

Engaged Communication – this is the minimum requirement – that there be open, honest, and intimate dialogue. We propose following the basic Communication Model described below – using it to dig deeply, and learn more of both "self" and "partner."

Engaged Contact – after the above is established, the couple creates levels of physical contact. It's essential to create flexible boundaries in this area, and to immediately discuss areas of confusion / discomfort.

Within the "safe hands" of Engaged Intimate, Relating anything is possible. We have the opportunity to trust, to open, to be vulnerable, and especially, to explore our own darkness, in the presence of a partner who is a curious, active participant.

The following 9 Tools form the basis for what is to follow – we believe that this is the only way to achieve personal and relational contentment!

As I noted earlier, this book is seemingly about relationships, but it's actually a self-development book. Self-work is the only way to engage with life, with others, and with our way of being. Our relationships shift precisely as much as we, as individuals, shift.

What follows are brief descriptions of the 9 Tools

I'll flesh them out in later chapters of this book. For now, let me suggest some understandings for each of these points,

The. Best. Relationship. Ever.

and how each applies to personal living and Elegant, Intimate Relating.

1. Total Honesty

It's impossible to have a rich and meaningful relationship while keeping secrets ("The flaw of omission,") or while lying ("The flaw of commission.")

Many are the excuses for dishonesty:

- "I'm an adult and I have a right to privacy."
- "(S)he might get mad if I was honest about everything."
- "I just want to be me – no need to talk about it."
- "White lies aren't harmful."

Being dishonest is a mini-betrayal. It's an indicator that you don't trust your partner enough to share what's up for you, and are embarrassed about your actions.

We advocate Total Honesty. And yes, sometimes being totally honest is scary, or might lead to a protracted discussion. But the truth is this: almost everyone who lies gets caught.

Personal: "It is my intention to tell the truth, all the time. I recognize that how "deeply I go" depends on who I'm interacting with, but I will answer truthfully, and be direct and clear with everyone."

Relational: "From this point on, my policy with you is Total Honesty. I'll let you know what I am thinking, how I am deciding, and what I am doing. I am not doing this for permission, but rather to foster intimacy and deepen our relationship. I invite you to do the same."

2. Being Present

Presence is about 2 things:

- being in the moment, the Now, and
- being focussed on what you are doing.

Most of us live our lives either in our heads (story-telling), or detached from our selves (numb.) Sort of ghosts, walking.

Being in the Now helps us to stay focussed on the immediate situation, while adding little or no drama through story-telling or future projections. This kind of presence allows us to deal with each situation as it occurs.

Personal: "I just tuned out and ended up imagining all kinds of stories that have nothing to do with the situation before me. I'll just have a breath and come back to the present moment."

Relational: "As I listened to you, I caught myself telling myself familiar stories about how hard-done-by I am. I recognize that my stories have nothing to do with you or the situation, so I'm filling you in as a way to come back to the Here and Now."

3. Being self-responsible

Self-responsibility is not about self-blame. Rather, it's about claiming ownership of our lives.

It is 'normal' to push responsibility away. Most are willing to take credit for success, and want to point a finger elsewhere when confronted with things judged 'wrong' or 'bad.'

Self-responsibility is simple – "I am the author of all of my life, as I view it right now." This is not a denial that 'bad' things happen," and that others may even intend us harm. It's to say that nothing compels us to act in ways that are non-helpful.

Personal: "This is going on right now, and I am making myself uncomfortable. Nevertheless, I am in this situation because of my choices. I can, at any time, choose differently."

Relational: "I am choosing to upset myself over the way I perceive our relationship. Therefore, I will own my responsibility for having gotten myself into the state I am in, and I will decide what I will do next."

4. Speaking clearly - Use dialogue to know yourself

We teach a specific Communication Model, and do so because most people are lousy communicators. Rather than use communication to deepen their self-understanding, they use it to justify their "hardened" behaviour and thinking, while proving others wrong. Or, they use communication to blame.

As soon as you harden a thought into a belief, you become less flexible and therefore less teachable, as you shift to, "I know, and I am right."

Dialogue, on the other hand, is about exploring our personal beliefs as we listen to feedback. It is essential to bear in mind that this exploration is only possible if you choose to hold your beliefs and "demands" loosely.

Personal: "Here is what I see, here is what I feel in my body, and here are the stories I am telling myself."

Relational: "I want to share with you my provisional guesses about what I see happening right now. I'm wondering about your perspectives on my stories – as I listen to you stating your perspectives on my story, I will not be defensive. I will listen with openness, and then clarify my intentions."

5. Being Curious – and NODing

When we live our lives up in our heads, dwelling on the past and fearing the future, we think that our version of misery is reality. We get locked into thought-loops. We exit the moment, shut down by tightening our bodies, and dwell in "Never-Never Land." The "Never" part is actually, "My life will never be different, and I'll never be able to change."

Curiosity is the opposite of self-righteousness and blame. If you pay attention, you'll notice that you are often confused about your own motivations and actions. How then, could you ever think you had a clue about what's up for others?

Personal: "I am drifting into past and future again. What is actually happening right now? Is anything required of me, right now? What does my body want to do? What would happen if I stopped telling myself stores, sat down, and had a breath?"

Relational: "When I confront situations like this one, I get caught in a mind loop... I'm wondering if you would have time to listen to my description, and then I'd like to hear about how you get yourself out of your mind-loops."

6. Letting go of Drama and Storytelling

Obviously, we have a **story** about ourselves – one we are anxious to tell others, and one we believe is 'true.' The story contains fragments of our biography, and mostly consists of examples that support our victim-story. One of the great leaps of self-responsibility is the understanding that our stories are "just stories."

The. Best. Relationship. Ever.

We have much invested in our life-story, and also give much energy to defending everything that props it up. We move past this by allowing ourselves to question both the accuracy and validity of the stories we are telling.

Letting go of **drama** is similar. Because we spend so much time talking to ourselves, about ourselves, we have a tendency to see ourselves as the centre of everything. Now, certainly, we are the centre of our own universe and experience – we're just not the centre of anything else. Despite our desire, no one is going to make us the centre of their universe. And the stuff that happens is the stuff that happens. It's not happening to you personally.

Personal: "Here is what is actually happening right now. I notice the story I'm struggling to tell, where I'm a poor, helpless victim, and I choose, this time, in this moment, to let that story go. In this moment, I'll be present and aware, and see what, if anything, is required of me."

Relational: "So, I notice that I'm hearing you speak, and I'm seeing what you're doing, and I'm telling myself all kinds of stories about how you are punishing me, or trying to manipulate me. I notice that I am creating these stories out of my thought-loops, and I want to acknowledge that I'm doing this. I will now let go, and return to being open and curious."

7. Being Flexible

The lynch-pin for Elegant, Intimate Relating is flexibility.

I may have spent years developing my relating style, but I also have the power, each time, to change what I am doing. In other words, I have a choice, *each time*, to do things differently, or to go back to habitual behaviour.

Integrity plays a big part here

While I know that I have complete freedom of expression, I also begin to look at the consequences (results) of my actions. I evaluate the result I am getting against what I have committed to – Elegant, Intimate Relating – and only do what deepens my relating.

This is flexibility

Personal: "Here I go again, doing the very things that endlessly land me in the soup. This is who I am, but right now, I can transform this pattern by stopping, having a breath, and making another choice."

Relational: "Wow, there I go again, blaming you for how I am feeling. I accept that I do this, and am pleasing myself that I caught myself this time. Give me a second to have a breath, and then I'll shift back to dialogue."

8. Feeling Your Feelings

Feelings have a bad reputation. People resist their 'negative' feelings – are caught in judgement – endlessly assigning "good / bad, right / wrong" categories to everything.

Essential to Elegant, Intimate Relating is total acceptance of each and every feeling

As we meditate, for example, what becomes clear is that thoughts and feelings flow through us like clouds crossing the sky. If we latch on to the feeling / thought, we create suffering for ourselves. If we express the thought or feeling, we can let it go.

There are no 'bad' feelings – there are, however, non-useful ways to express them. So, we accept and transform each feeling by expressing it with awareness.

The. Best. Relationship. Ever.

Personal: "I am aware of my anger, my boredom, my sexuality and sensuality, my tightness, my shutting down – all of my feelings. I accept that these feelings pass through me – they are not me, but rather expressions of my moment-by-moment experience. I therefore choose to express them safely and thoroughly."

Relational: "I'm noticing that [the current feelings] are coming up for me, and I'm wondering if you'd be interested in helping me to fully experience and express them, so that I can learn their lesson and then move on to whatever is next." (see below, Expressing your Feelings)

9. Exploring Sensuality and Sexuality

Most adults have "issues" around open, honest, and deep revelation and expression of matters sexual. The discomfort is deep-seated – stretching back to childhood.

Because of our discomfort, we talk in euphemisms and hints. We tend to only get part of what we are looking for, and might be unclear about what we want.

We also have desires and attractions for others, and are uncomfortable both with the feelings themselves, and with sharing them. We avoid conversations about our "turn-ons," out of confusion, fear, and to avoid jealousy. We end up more confused, blocked, and wary.

Personal: "I am doing some serious work exploring my sensual and sexual nature. I am going to use clear language to describe who I am and what I want sexually, and I am going to create "Vulnerability Projects" to explore areas I am curious about / scare myself over."

Relational: "I am noticing that I have some issues as regards my sensuality / sexuality. I am exploring these issues, and I will keep you informed about what I am discovering, as well as invite you to work on some of this with me. I also commit to keeping you updated on people I am relating with, and letting you know who I find attractive, chargy, etc."

Let's see how this all plays out.

Chapter Five: Total Honesty

About Total Honesty, and why you need to adopt it

Darbella and I have only one relationship "rule" – total honesty. We set that up back when we first started dating. It keeps things simple. We do as we choose to, and keep each other completely informed.

Total Honesty means stating what you are thinking and feeling as things occur to you. You keep your partner informed about your life experiences – about friends, attractions, issues and problems, and about money, your family, – about everything.

The Line in the Sand

A line in the sand is something that happens that becomes "the deal-breaker" for your relationship. Ideally, the list of "lines" ought to be quite short. Also, those few items ought to be "big." As opposed to a client who ended her marriage because her husband forgot to clean the sink. No. Really.

Many couples have not actually sat down, discussed, and agreed upon their line(s) in the sand. If they did, they'd likely discover that there are a few "biggies," and a ton of dumb things, like:

- "If you look at another (wo)man, I'll leave you."
- "If you yell at me one more time, I'll leave you."

Examples like these are the adult equivalent of the six-year-old having a fit, stamping his feet and screaming, "I hate you! I'm running away from home!"

Also, if you are just threatening to leave and don't when something happens, you are lying. This makes the line in the sand an empty threat.

The Alternative to Total Honesty is Secrets – otherwise known as lying

In order to lie to another, I first have to lie to myself.

- For children, the "self-lie" is: "If I lie, I'll get away with this."
- For adults, the "self-lie" is: "He'll only get mad if I tell the truth, so I'm lying to make it easier on him. Besides, I'm an adult, and some stuff should just be kept private!"

The cosmic joke about lying is two-fold: we mostly get caught in our lies, and even if we don't, lying always damages the relationship.

I once worked with a highly dysfunctional teen. She described her lying process: "I decided that I'd never tell my parents the truth. So, I lie, and then I lie about lying, and I keep doing it until I can't remember the lies, and then I get caught, and I cry and say I'll never do it again, which, of course, is the first lie in the next series."

And she said all of this with a straight face and a slight smile. This sounds like the approach to honesty of many of my clients who are in dysfunctional relationships.

The. Best. Relationship. Ever.

"Our line in the sand is total honesty"

Elegant, Intimate Relating begins when we stop lying to ourselves. In a sense, the "Total Honesty policy" is not about the other person. I'm not choosing to be honest for Dar's sake. I'm being honest for my sake.

The decision to be honest comes from a place of integrity. If I have chosen to do something, and "believe in" the something I'm doing, then I 'need to' be honest about it.

The reason we either lie, or don't tell our partner about something we thought or did, (a "lie of omission") is because we fear the consequences of the behaviour we are lying about.

I know lots of business people who would never cheat a client on a business deal, but endlessly "cheat" in their personal lives.

I don't mean "cheating" as in "having an affair," (although having an affair and *not telling your partner* is a violation of Total Honesty.) I'm not condemning extra-marital affairs. I have no judgement at all about them.

I'm defining "cheating" this way: "Cheating is not being scrupulously honest about what you are doing." It's not "cheating," nor lying, if I am doing something and being totally honest with my partner about what I am doing.

The only Truth I can tell is "The truth as I know it Today"

Sometimes, I change my mind. I may decide to do 'x' one day, and then go do it, and decide that the next time I'll do 'y.'

As long as I'm keeping Dar totally in the loop, and letting her know any changes in my thinking about the topic, I might be *inconsistent* but certainly not lying.

And if you think about it, the actual "truth" of such a situation would be, "I'm thinking several things about this, am not sure, and am trying out different behaviours, while keeping you informed."

Finally, what's included in the "honesty" pact? Everything.

Anytime you might think to exclude something, don't. Tell each other everything.

Total Honesty requires elegant communication. (see: Speaking Clearly) So, how we say what we say is also relevant, and totally under our control.

I don't remember what the disagreement was about, but one evening Dar and I were on about something, and I remember, clearly, choosing to annoy the hell out of myself.

I remember thinking, "You know, I really am feeling cold and distant from Dar." (Again, see Speaking Clearly.) I knew that I could say that, in those words, and Dar would accept it as an honest statement of fact.

Instead, my perverse side said, "She's got the audacity to argue with you! Make her hurt!" I know Darbella, and, I thought I knew what to say.

I looked her in the eyes, put a bit of surliness in my voice, and said, "You know, I feel absolutely nothing for you right now."

The. Best. Relationship. Ever.

For a few seconds, my words had their intended effect. Dar then said, "Nice try. I'm not going to hurt myself over that."

Being honest, I said, "I made a decision to say that in a way you might hurt yourself over. I was looking to hurt, not communicate."

With this kind of dialogue, our disagreements have been short-lived.

Total Honesty helps us to think about the intention of our words and actions. If my intent is to blame or hurt, I want to be honest and say that this is my intention.

If my intent is to communicate, I'll speak in a way that will facilitate my partner actually hearing what I'm saying.

Elegant communication and transparent Total Honesty is the name of the game if I choose to live my life with skill and passion.

"It is my intention and practice to be Totally Honest with you. I'm not going to lie to you, no matter what. I am not "protecting" you by being dishonest, and any other story I tell myself to continue being dishonest is not helpful.

I invite you to join me in a Total Honesty project. Total Honesty is so important to me that I consider it [a, the] line in the sand for me."

Chapter Six: Being Present

"The world we see that seems so insane is the result of a belief system that is not working. To perceive the world differently, we must be willing to change our belief system, let the past slip away, expand our sense of now, and dissolve the fear in our minds." ~ William James

The world has always seemed insane

In the midst of crazy, there is always the choice to be open. And to be open, we have to:

- notice where we are, and
- bring ourselves to presence

We've talked about the movies in our heads, and how much credence we give to them. I mentioned how each of us has a story about "my perfect partner," against which we compare real people.

One 26-year-old I occasionally work with has a ton of stories about herself and the men she dates. One story is, "If I have sex with a guy I pick up in a bar, he'll eventually want to date me and marry me." (Because of course that's why guys pick up girls in bars…)

Another of her stories: "I'm lazy. I think I'll just keep doing what I've been doing, despite never having had a long-term relationship that worked."

The. Best. Relationship. Ever.

She has entire movies built on these models. After another failure, she gets inspired to do away with the stories, the movies. Then, after a week or so, sighs, and says, "It's too hard. I shouldn't have to work this hard." And she goes back to doing what doesn't work.

This is insane, but hey, pretty common

What's nuts is her belief system. And even more important, it's nuts that she prefers her plainly faulty belief system to the reality of hard work and another approach.

In short, she believes:

- Picking up guys in bars leads to marriage
- Having sex with guys leads to intimacy in other areas
- Guys only want her because she's "hot"
- She's lazy, so she'll do more of what doesn't work, and expects to get different results

You must learn your physical signals

Every item in the Tools section of this book references your feelings. By feelings, I mean the actual sensations in your body. (See Speaking Clearly.) Mostly we just react to stuff, and "miss" that our bodies are uncomfortable when we are making messes.

In order to stay present, figure out what "absent" feels like

Absent is any time we are up in our heads, storytelling. It's regretting the past, it's worrying about the future, and it's also imagining, as opposed to *having*, experiences.

Your job is to find the "feel" of "story-ville" – to learn your physical and mental cues for zoning out and living in your head.

The reason we need to do this should be obvious

Think back to Sam and Sally. Virtually all of their misery was caused by both of them refusing to discuss or experience the moment at hand. Both left the present moment (the discussion) and both dredged up an old story. They refused to shift their stories – both chose to condemn the other for not living up to the fiction in their heads.

Here are a few concepts from the William James quote above

1) James – "The world we see that seems so insane is the result of a belief system that is not working."

Everything you see in your life is caused by you – caused by your beliefs and your choices. If you are alone, that's you, making "alone" happen. If you are angry, that's you, creating anger. If you are unfulfilled, that's about you and your choices. And on and on, up the scale, to "all of it." Stomping your feet and screaming, "It's not fair!" accomplishes precisely nothing, and no one cares.

What to do:

- Learn what non-presence (your disconnect) feels like to you, and
- Make a pact with your partner to notice non-presence in each other, and to encourage each other to come back into the Here and Now.

Your partner likely has a pretty good idea when you shift into "story-telling." You know when your partner shifts, too. So, make it a practice to talk about what you feel when

- your partner goes away, and
- when you do.

The. Best. Relationship. Ever.

"I have a queasy feeling in my stomach, and I notice that your eyes are looking away. The story I'm telling myself is that you are up in your head, telling yourself stories, and therefore aren't present with me. I am wondering if that fits for you, and if so, if you'd like to re-establish contact with me, and also share your stories."

"I just want to check in with you. I just noticed that I was up in my head comparing you with my stories, and getting ready to pick a fight. I'm back now, I apologise for checking out, and I'd like to tell you my stories, and then suggest some ideas regarding the actual situation."

2) James – "To perceive the world differently, we must be willing to change our belief system…"

It is impossible to change someone else's belief system. All you can do is change yours. You then act from the new belief, resisting the urge to fall back into old stories and behaviours. And, in dialogue, you invite your partner to explore their belief system.

A client, a few weeks ago, had a pretty dramatic Bodywork session – lots of feelings and emotions and dramas surfaced, and she worked her way through all of it. As she made direct eye contact, she said, "I'm so present!"

I email my Bodywork clients the following day, and ask, "How are you, and how is your body? What's come up for you?" I do this because profound shifting often takes place – it's good to notice and acknowledge it.

She wrote back something to the tune of: "I'm taking today to recover."

I replied:

"Why would you want to re-cover, after making such progress un-covering?"

Recovering

I was making a little joke – I was thinking that re-covering describes our urge to go back to non-presence, so we can resurrect our old stories. We "cover ourselves again in our old story."

Your Ego is totally and completely invested in keeping you "safe" (stuck in old stories) and it does this by endlessly bitching at you – trying to scare you. Egos fear change, and rebel at doing things differently.

Our Egos demand that we return to our "past dignity" by re-covering ourselves in the lies that have never worked, and have made us the miserable, shut down creatures that led us to seek change in the first place!

You are where you are because of the power of your beliefs. Getting somewhere else requires – demands – changing both your belief system and your behaviour

> So: "I'm noticing that as I see this situation differently, I also notice a real pull to go back up into my head do what I have always done – start blaming you. I also notice a pull to get all self-righteous, and also to yell at myself. I'm checking in with you to report all of this. Also, my chest is tight, so would you please apply some pressure to my sternum?" (see Feeling Your Feelings.)

3) James – "…let the past slip away…"

This is tough, because we are so invested in our stories. We just know we were abused, persecuted, held down, and

The. Best. Relationship. Ever.

held back – judged and found wanting. We just know that we're always going to be alone, or always be with idiots, or always be stuck in whatever we believe is the substance of our self-generated quicksand.

And yet, all of that "knowing" is just your story, and not a very helpful one

Letting the past slip away means loosening your grip on the 'facts.' You do this by recognizing that you are the sole author of your story, and you chose what aspects to focus on.

The TV show "24" shot 26 *hours* of film for every one hour segment. The director and the editors took the 26 hours of film and boiled it down to a one hour, real-time segment.

Now, think. How many possible plot points, perspectives, and directions are contained in that 26 hours of film? It's infinite. Yet, once it's edited and "in the can," it's condensed down to only one version. And, get this. The scenes chosen, out of endless possibilities, matches the predetermined script!

This is what we do, all the time, as we review every instance (plot-point) in our long lives. We edit, we ignore stuff, we stitch together unrelated events, and we tell ourselves that the concoction is "my life."

However, it's a story. Out of all of the myriad facts of our life, we have edited what "the facts" to fit our "script." We can't stop doing this... but we can notice and acknowledge it.

We recognize it, and let it go.

"I'm noticing that I'm dredging up one of my favourite victim stories, and I just wanted to let you know I'm doing that. I may need to [pound a mattress, cry, yell, take a walk, etc.] and

then I want to get back to what we were actually talking about."

4) James – "…expand our sense of now…"

All of your stories, your movies, are in your head until you die. The letting go just described is actually a turning away from. In other words, it's not about reconstructing a better story, or not having stories at all (impossible!).

It's about living in the Here and Now

Being present is having a love affair with Now. The "24" illustration is important. It explains why you can go through a situation with someone, and when discussing it, hear two different stories.

It's not that one story is 'true,' and the other 'false.' It's that each person filters the data (chooses the 'right' scenes out of all the scenes filmed) through their expectations (their script.)

The Here and Now, on the other hand, is just what it is. If we treat our experiences as "unique moments," then what we find is the flexibility to respond without the drama of the past or the fear of the future muddying the waters.

"I notice I'm distracting myself with my stories, so just give me a second while I breathe. [Shut up, focus on your breath, and take several calming breaths.] OK, I'm back – Here and Now – let's continue."

5) James – "…and dissolve the fear in our minds."

Fear is unreal. Situations aren't intrinsically scary – the reality is that we sometimes choose to scare ourselves about a situation. The fear, then, is in our heads.

The. Best. Relationship. Ever.

Fear is caused by our internal stories. If you are fearful, you are not present. When you are present and aware, there is no time for fear. We dissolve fear by calming ourselves, turning our eyes away from the story to the reality of the moment, and then choosing.

Practically, our relationships fail because our fear of intimacy, honesty, and vulnerability (or better, or fear of the results) leads us to shut down, lie, withhold, and blame. But we're doing all of this internally – creating the fear, and then choosing to let it dictate our behaviour.

Shifting back into presence takes courage. You decide to be present, and then you do it. You peel away the phony layers of protection, open yourself up, and let others see who you are. You become open, honest, and vulnerable, because you want to step out of the games, into the light of who you actually are.

Decide to engage with your intimate partners openly. The best way to do this is to open yourself physically. Here's how:

Sit, give yourself a shake, breathe deeply and often, and let your body relax.

If you cross your legs, place your ankle on your knee. You don't want your thighs together. This posture opens the belly. We know that "belly open" = openness and vulnerability.

If your feet are on the floor, then knees and thighs apart.

Uncross your arms. No hugging yourself. Chest open, shoulders comfortably back, no tightness. This is one physical sign of open-heartedness and vulnerability – of having the courage to share your vulnerability.

Your eyes are open and focussed on your partner, mostly on your partner's eyes. You can widen your field of view to see how your partner is holding herself. But mostly, your open eyes are looking at your partner's eyes.

As you open your eyes, heart, belly, and knees, you will find yourself, and be more accessible for sharing who you are and where you are. You will be present, aware, un-covered, and unafraid.

Chapter Seven: Being Self-responsible

My favourite TV show, now cancelled, was "Lie to Me." The show was loosely based upon the work of Paul Eckman, a psychologist who studies facial expression, emotion, and deception. I suggest you have a look at the book "*Emotional Awareness*," which is a dialogue between Eckman and the Dalai Lama.

The book, and Eckman's work, is a vital read, as it documents the process we all go through as we experience emotions. Emotions are a part of our internal wiring – indeed, certain emotional reactions seem hard-coded prior to birth, as anyone who has seen a red-faced newborn screaming at the top of her lungs can attest.

Here's an example: how "fear – threat" hard-wiring saves our life

Eckman describes this familiar scene: you're driving along, and you spot a car heading right for you, and quickly. (This is the stimulus.) In micro-seconds, your body reacts (the reaction) by turning the wheel, hitting the brakes, etc. At the same time the emotion "fear" arises, and with it, physiological changes such as holding your breath, blood rushing to your hands, etc.

Assuming you survive, an "emotional let-down" occurs. You might shake, grow pale, etc. This is the emotion, (and adrenalin) dissipating.

Every aspect of that happened on auto-pilot.

You experienced the hard-wired, mysterious workings of the "fear - threat sensor," which decided that a fast moving object was going to hit you.

Eckman says that we are scanning for such events all the time, and that we've survived as a species because of our almost instantaneous reactions.

Now, remember, cars have only existed for 100 years or so, so the instinct to avoid *a car* is a learned behaviour that was tacked onto our original "avoid the tiger" program. While base reactions are hard-wired, we also learn to integrate new situations.

The other key point: this reaction has to be absolutely, positively automatic. We end up dead if we start thinking, at all, about car-accident-avoidance.

The first issue happens when this fear-avoidance-process is improperly applied within our relationships.

There is a second issue

Eckman describes how, when in the throes of any emotion, our brains shut off (so that we stop thinking and just react.) The brain selectively registers only input and memories that confirm and support the present emotion. We become locked in to the story we are telling ourselves. This keeps the emotion alive well past it's "due date."

The. Best. Relationship. Ever.

And a third issue

The fear-stimulus itself (the situation) might be forgotten. It drops out of our awareness – and we are left with the emotion – we are "enraged," or "grief-stricken." We've "forgotten" why, and we seem to have no options.

Hopeless, right?

Well, no. Much of Eckman's dialogue with the Dalai Lama revolves around finding a way out of this seemingly automatic process.

I call the way out "Being Self-responsible"

Being self-responsible first of all requires a commitment to do things differently. We stop one behaviour, and substitute another. There's nothing, however, simple about actually doing it.

You may think, "Wouldn't it be wonderful to keep the automatic "car reaction," and get rid of automatic "yelling at the wife or husband" reaction." That's impossible! The triggering process happens in a heart-beat. Something is said or done, and we find ourselves "in our emotions."

There is no way to avoid this initial spike of rising emotions. In chosen situations, (like with our partner, or with people in general,) however, I believe we can drive a wedge (I'm going to call this "the gap,") between feeling the emotion and our subsequent behaviour – our reaction – or simply put, what we do next.

The Dalai Lama mentions meditation as one way to learn to create "the gap" between emotion and action, and being a meditator, I agree.

However, I learned to create "the gap" prior to establishing a meditation practice. What is required is acknowledging our issue, (see NODing,) discovering our internal feelings when triggered, and enacting the substitute behaviour. More on this below.

At this phase of our work, you must decide – are you going to make excuses, or begin to enact a different way of being, through self-responsibility?

If you choose Elegant, Intimate Relating, you must let go of your defensiveness, and let go of declaring some aspects of your behaviour "fixed in stone."

We are excellent at finding evidence for our preconceived notions

If I believe that I was victimized in the past, and also believe that I have no choice but to stay a victim now, all I will see are things that support my belief. If I think someone behaves badly, all I will see is bad behaviour. If I believe that I am depressed, or manic, or confused, or stupid, I will see endless examples supporting my belief.

You escape this trap by becoming aware of the games you play with yourself, and accepting that it is, indeed, you that is playing with you. Once you make this leap, which requires learning your own patterns and also feeling your defensiveness, you begin living self-responsibly. I call this, "Exercising control over the method of expression of emotions, through self-responsibility."

I'm going to tell you a couple of stories about how I discovered this. First, want to say a word about addiction.

The. Best. Relationship. Ever.

Anger and Addiction

My stories concern how I learned to deal differently with my temper – my angry outbursts. The issue was not the angry feeling – it was how I chose to express it. This was my big issue for the first 32 years of my life.

Until I decided that I could create "the gap," I argued loudly that there was absolutely nothing I could do about my hot temper.

This is the same as being addicted to, for example, alcohol. Before a person stops drinking, they believe that, as it says in the First Step of AA, "We admitted we were powerless over alcohol–that our lives had become unmanageable."

Now, it gets interesting. In AA, the next step is to turn to, "...a Power greater than ourselves [that] could restore us to sanity."

My belief is that the power that "restores us" is our own internal commitment to change

The person hits "rock bottom," acknowledges the addiction, admits to both having it and being powerless to prevent it, and then, finds a tool or tools to divert the addiction to drinking.

In AA, the tools are meetings, sponsors, and emphatically, finding the means not to take the *next* drink. In other words, there is no commitment to never drinking again – the commitment is to not drink this time (in this Here and Now moment.)

I believe that people who quit drinking are not special – they are normal humans who reached a point of such focus (or desperation) that they created "the gap" – they committed to practicing a new way of being.

• • •

Speaking Clearly

OK, so here's how this works in Elegant, Intimate Relating

Self-responsibility comes from acknowledging and accepting that many of your relating skills simply and plainly suck. And that includes enacting your emotions "at" your partner. (see "About" vs. "At.")

Following your acknowledgement, (no excuses! This is what you are doing!) you make the crucial decision:

"From now on, when my emotions arise, I am going to create "the gap" between emotion and reaction. I am going to study myself. I am going to learn to feel and identify my emotions as they arise. I will use the self-discipline of "non-reaction," and then choose an elegant response."

And then you do it. Again and again.

Let me tell you my story

I grew up in a tough part of Buffalo, NY, and learned to defend myself with my mouth first, then my fists. I was so good with my mouth that I seldom had to fight, but I was always ready.

At 31, in my first year of training to be a therapist, because of my verbal "skills," I get pigeon-holed into the role of, "He who destroys the work of the other Interns." I quite got off on the power and prestige.

Needless to say, this attitude and approach of being the critic and "always right," leached into all of my intimate relationships.

In my last year, I decided to look at my big mouth and angry responses, and my therapist encouraged me to do more than look. I decided to figure out a way to stop my

The. Best. Relationship. Ever.

mouth, and see what happened. I created "the gap," and applied it – I called it biting my tongue.

I made it 3 years without slipping – I was at a meeting, a guy challenged me quite aggressively, and "had a relapse." Instantaneously, I was back to attack dog mode.

I ripped the guy a new one, and sat back, satisfied. I was devastated when the rest of the group got up and surrounded the other guy, and called me heartless. That was April of 1986, and I haven't slipped again. (I still *think* angry words, though!)

Story 2

I was for a while a minister, and there was a guy in one of my congregations who was a recovering addict and abuser – big mouth, small brain. One day in 1994, he decided to offend himself over something he thought I'd said or implied. He "invited" me back into the sanctuary, slammed the door shut, and got "up in my face." Bulging eyes, clenched fists, spittle flying, the whole thing.

Here is what happened, for me:

- 1) Initially, as I heard his volume and observed him angering himself, (the stimulus) I involuntarily took a step back, my breathing stopped, and I noticed my legs were burning, my jaw was aching, and I was starting to ball my fists (the instantaneous physical reaction.)
- 2) A second later, my brain exploded with ANGER! "How dare he! If he touches me, I'll kill him!" All declared loudly, in my head, and with a lot of profanity. I was enraging myself! (The emotion.)
- 3) I then felt a sort of "thunk" inside of me, as "the gap" I had created caused a door to close, effectively barring me from expressing the emotion. In that instant, I heard, in-

Speaking Clearly

ternally, my calm voice, saying, "He is not allowed to touch you. He can say whatever he wants."
- 4) I simultaneously relaxed my hands, planted my feet, and said, "Tell me more."

He yelled at me for about 20 minutes. I listened, commented calmly, and asked questions (you'll hear more about these skills in the next chapter...) He wound down, and we found a way to end the event.

Let me say clearly that the entire time, my guts were churning, and my "Kill him!" internal voice was droning in the background.

I believe I was able to make the choices I made in this (so far) once-in-a-lifetime event because I'd been practicing creating "the gap," instance by instance, for many, many years.

My day-to-day practice prepared me for this confrontation. And as they say, the lessons do get harder as we learn more!

Oh, and I did go home and pound the crap out of my bed, and did a lot of yelling and swearing, but none of it was aimed at him.

So, here's the plan: How to create "the gap" through self-responsible behaviour

- 1) Talk with friends, people you're in relationship with, relatives, and ask them to help you to identify what you do that gets in the way of your relating. Ask them which emotions you toss into the mix – especially emotions you claim you cannot control.
- 2) Sit with your principal partner and make a commitment to "create a gap" between the arising of an emotion, and your former automatic response. You might, as I did, decide to just shut up for a bit, and unclench yourself.

The. Best. Relationship. Ever.

- 3) Use the Communication Model (next chapter) to describe your process, (the emotional reaction you are working on,) again without enacting the emotion.
- 4) Declare a "rule" – "I will not express emotions "at" living things. I will discuss, and also will express my emotions safely." (see Feeling Your Feelings)

Remember: Emotions are auto-reactions to externals. How you choose to *respond* to an emotion is totally yours, even if you don't presently see "the gap."

In other words, keeping with anger, no one 'makes' me angry. People do whatever they do, and I react to the stimulus, anger myself (or sadden myself, or amuse myself...)

Then, if I choose self-responsibility, I implement "the gap," I get off of auto-pilot, and choose my next behaviour.

This is "owning" your anger (see NODing)

As for the anger itself, you choose to safely and cleanly express it by aiming it at an inanimate object. I therefore do not yell *at* Darbella. I invite her to be a witness as I yell at a chair, a tree (we used to own property with a small bush) – I'd stand up, nude, in the hot tub and scream at the trees in the woods –a sight to behold!)

I may also pound a heavy bag or the bed, or the seat of a chair.

The idea is to 'have' the emotion. Not justify the emotion, explain the emotion, or blame someone for the emotion. Have it. Express it. Move through the emotion.

This applies, of course, to all emotions. When sad, one cries. When in need of support, one asks for a hug. All of the "problems with emotions" go away when I accept responsibility for controlling the *expression* of my emotions. (again, see Feeling your Feelings.)

Chapter Eight: Speaking clearly - Using dialogue to know yourself

Effective Communication through dialogue is not an inborn skill. It's actually a "foreign language."

- For most couples, what passes for communication is often better described as a simultaneous monologue.
- Most couples have problems communicating because they have grown up witnessing *poor* communication. They hear adults speaking from a place of **self-righteousness**. They hear about wounded feelings, which are blamed on the behaviour of *other people* or *external situations*.

Effective communication is not:

- getting another person to agree with you
- teaching, explaining, or lecturing
- manipulating another person into doing things your way
- bargaining, cajoling, or begging

Effective communication *is*:

- clearly differentiating between thoughts and feelings
- using self-responsible language exclusively
- honestly stating what you know about *your* thoughts and feelings
- remaining present (in the Here and Now,) so as to resist the urge to blame

- speaking with compassionate, total honesty

The Nuts and Bolts of Effective Communication

Darbella and I use a modification of what's called the "Haven Communication Model." The Haven Model pretty well matches the original Couples Communication model I learned as a "baby therapist in training," back in 1982.

I've sketched out both models, showing the older terms in italics, and the Haven terms in regular text. For now, just notice that the five "elements" are the same size. I'll be coming back to that below, as I redraw the Model, and explain the elements in detail.

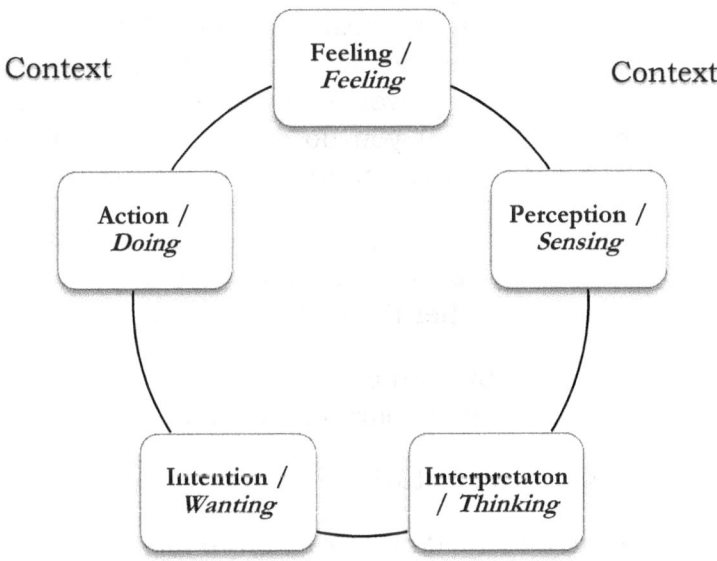

Terms in italics - *Awareness Wheel* – Couple Communication, 1979

Terms in standard font – *Haven Model* –Wong & McKeen 1992

The. Best. Relationship. Ever.

I think that the two "hardest parts" of any communication model are,

- learning the difference between a feeling and an interpretation, and
- doing what you say you will do. (action)

The difference between a feeling and an interpretation

Feelings Are Just That

Here's a 100% rule for you: Everything that is going on inside of you is about you, or better put, is "caused" by you.

The Buddhist concept of emptiness speaks to this – empty means, "empty of any intrinsic meaning." Using the illustration of speech, what someone says to you is nothing more than sonic vibrations. The words themselves do not intrinsically carry meaning. What you do with the sound (how you interpret it – ascribe meaning to it) is 100% up to you.

We ascribe meaning to everything, and typically make what's happening fit our preconceived notions. It's not the words that hurt, but rather the spin we put on them.

In terms of the 100% rule, what I feel as I communicate is caused by me, not by my partner's words.

Here's an example, featuring Sam and Sally.

Sally says to Sam, "You never listen to me!"

Key point: Sally's intention in saying this is immaterial to Sam's response – despite Sally's intention; the words only mean what Sam makes of them.

What happens is this: the electrical signals that represent Sally's words reach Sam's brain. At that instant, Sam's brain simultaneously defines the words, (decides who "you" is, remembers what "never" means, etc.) and interprets (ascribes his own meaning and intention.) He may also feel a feeling.

All of that is Sam's doing, and has everything to do with who Sam is, how he was brought up, and what his level of self-awareness is.

- If Sam is *normal,* (meaning inept at communication...) Sam will *react* instead of *responding.* For example:
- He might flatly deny what he *judges* (or interprets) to be an accusation. "Of course I listen to you, you never shut up!"
- Or, Sam might specifically challenge the word "never." "I spent an hour listening to you this morning!"
- Or, he might go on the offensive. "What you mean I don't listen? You never listen to me! And besides, we haven't had sex in a week!"
- He might try to shift blame to Sally. Sam might say, "You are making me sad." Sam declares himself to be a victim, and the conversation gets derailed – Sam and Sally end up talking about Sam's sadness. Or, they end up arguing about whether making Sam sad was Sally's intent. In either case, Sally's poorly expressed issue – that she thinks that she is not being heard – is forgotten.

If Sam is a self-responsible person, he would do two things:

- *First*, he would describe his internal experience.
- *Second*, he would express curiosity.

A Feeling is an Internal Experience

Definition: a feeling has to be felt in the body. Thus, "I feel you don't understand me" is NOT a feeling; it's an interpretation, and is spoken as, "My interpretation (the story I am telling myself) is that you do not understand me." The feeling is spoken as, "I'm feeling tight, cold, and distant from you."

Let's try the example again. Sally says to Sam, "You never listen to me!"

Sam might say, "As I hear you say that, I feel cold and distant from you." Notice that Sam uses self-responsible language to own his feelings. There is a very practical reason for doing this. It encourages dialogue, as opposed to arguing.

The self-responsible person uses "I" language to describe their internal, self-created "feeling-state." "Here is who I am, and here is what's up for me."

Sam might then shift to his interpretations.

Darbella and I love to use the following clause – "So, the story I'm telling myself is..." You could substitute "My judgement..." or "My interpretation..." for "The story I'm telling myself..."

Sam: "So, the story I'm telling myself is that you're trying to pick a fight – and I am making myself anxious, and I'm judging that you no longer love me."

Now, while the language may seem a bit kludgy, this is precisely what's going on inside of Sam, and it's devoid of any blame directed at Sally.

Curiosity

If Sam is wise, having expressed what's up for him, he might remember where the conversation started. Sally was raising an issue about *thinking* that she was unheard. (Remember, you can't "feel" unheard – it's an interpretation, not a feeling.)

Sam might say,

"As I hear you say that, I feel cold and distant from you. The story I'm telling myself is that you're trying to pick a fight – and I am making myself anxious, and I'm judging that you no longer love me. However, I'm curious about what you think I'm not hearing."

This is an open invitation for Sally to share more information.

If Sally is wise, she hears what Sam is saying – that he's describing his internal experience without blame. This creates space for Sally to have a breath, as opposed to getting defensive.

Then, she hears his statement of curiosity.

The curiosity question is a very clear mirror – "Here is what I heard – please tell me more." And it's called mirroring because it acts like a mirror – the reflection in a mirror is neither more, nor less, than the object reflected.

Now, some of you are going to want to argue that real people don't talk like this – that fighting and arguing and name-calling are the basis of relating. In the words of Dr. Phil, all I can say is, "How's that working for you?"

The only thing the "normal approach" gets you is more of the same – resentment, more fights, the silent treatment, anger, drama.

If that's what you want, by all means keep doing it. Or, you could grow up, and get over yourself.

The. Best. Relationship. Ever.

More on Feelings and Interpretations

I was talking with a client recently who said, "Yesterday was a really anxious day." I replied, "Days aren't anxious, so you might put it, 'I made myself anxious yesterday.'"

As she was lying face down for Bodywork at the time, she rapidly pushed herself up into what would be called, in yoga, the Cobra Pose, her face filled with disbelief.

She said, "All my life, I've believed that there are good days and bad days – that externals cause feelings. You're saying I caused my anxiety!"

I replied, "Not quite. You felt something in your body, and interpreted it as anxiety. Declaring yourself (or the day!) anxious is a thought. What were you actually feeling in your body?"

She said, "My muscles were really tight, and I wasn't breathing much... holy crap, that fits! I almost never breathe very much!"

I then said, "Right. The feeling is tight and breathless. That feeling leads to the thought (interpretation), "I am anxious." In actuality, you could call the tight and breathless feeling in your body anything you chose. It's just a label."

So what's the point?

Well, people use their feelings as bludgeons – they suggest, and none too subtly, that others are the cause – are to blame – for their poor little pitiful feelings. So, I work really hard to get people to own their bodily sensations, while also owning the stories they tell themselves about those sensations.

If I say, "Here is the story I'm inventing regarding the tight feeling in my stomach," I am accepting total self-responsibility for both the feeling and the interpretation.

Whatever is going on in your head is just your story

What you believe about how you were parented, what you believe about past relationships, what you believe about your child rearing skills, what you believe about your employment – it's all just you talking to yourself.

Believing interpretations are 'real' is what gets people in trouble

They get an idea about a situation, or an illness, or a person, and they not only believe that idea is true, they demand that others believe it too. They ascribe all kinds of meaning to what other people are doing, with no data other than the stories they've invented in their heads. They have all kinds of reasons and justifications for staying stuck, and get quite incensed when someone suggests they drop the nonsense and do something different.

In order to be an effective communicator, you must learn to differentiate between thoughts (interpretations) and feelings!

Read the above sections several times, and practice, practice, practice!

The. Best. Relationship. Ever.

All About Action

I recently decided to redraw the Communication Model:

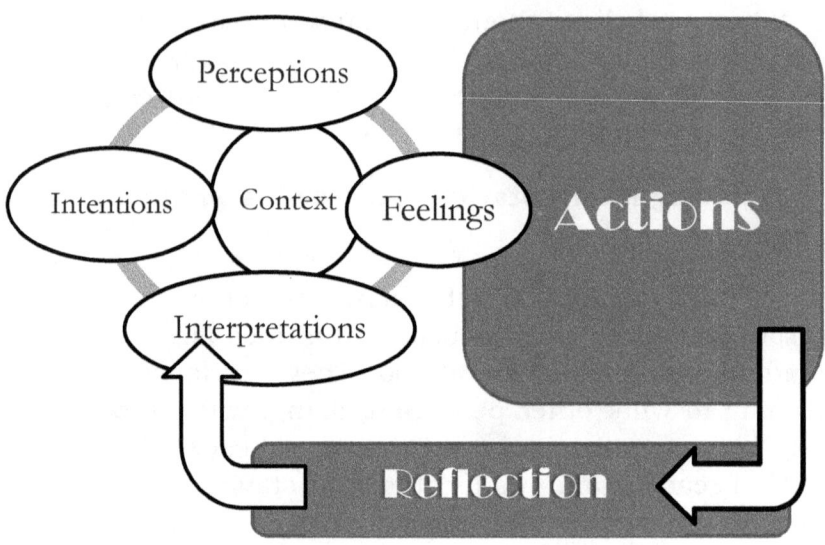

As might be obvious, I have made **Action** equal in size to the rest of the model; as opposed to the same size as the other segments (see the Haven Model, above.) I am convinced that the key to Elegant, Intimate Relating is precisely the action – what I do.

Here's the point: you've got to choose a new way of relating, and then… do it! More on this below.

This is Integrity

I define integrity as: "My behaviour matches my words, without excuse or exception." Thus, we move out of integrity by coming up with either an excuse or an exception.

Excuses are pointers to "things I declare to be out of my control":

- "My father always yelled, so I can't help myself."
- "My son is not living up to his potential, so I have to lecture him, for his own good."
- "Everyone knows that women get cranky and emotional this time of the month."

Exceptions are created by making the present circumstance something special, as in,

- "I know I said I would not yell at my kids, but this time they were so bad I just had to."
- "I know I said I wouldn't drink when I had a bad day, but this day was so bad I just had to drink."

Integrity based living is doing what you say, all the time. It's essential to keep "doing vs. promising" at the forefront, as we define the other aspects of the Communication Model.

The elements of the Communication Model

Context

Context is the "stuff" we bring to the present situation. Context describes all of our experience. Our context is informed by both our upbringing and our immediate and past history.

Context includes:

- Stereotypes: who is in charge, who is of value, what is important
- Bias: good vs. bad, significant vs. insignificant

The. Best. Relationship. Ever.

- Family of Origin dynamics: the way the parents communicated with each other and with their children – the household "rules," etc.
- History: not the actual details, but rather the story you choose to tell about what you think you remember. **History includes everything,** *including* "today's drive home from work."

Perceptions:

Sensory data: the 5 senses: what you hear and see, what you feel "on your skin," and what you smell and taste. If you are sighted, most of what you report under this category is, "Here is what I see you doing" followed by, "And this is what I heard you say."

- "I notice that your arms are crossed, and you are looking down."
- "I notice that your tone of voice has changed." (There is no interpretation here, no, "Your voice just got bitchy.")
- "As you finished that thought, you sighed."

Feelings: (Internal sensations)

- Warm / cold
- Open / closed (or shut down)
- Attracted / repelled
- Comfortable / uncomfortable
- Tight / loose
- Full / empty
- Close / distant

Feelings are "a physical sensation, going on inside." This differs from what I feel externally: "Silk feels soft on my skin." (That would be reported under perceptions, as silk on skin might be painful to a burn victim.)

Learning to "feel what we are feeling" takes a bit of effort. Most of my clients initially have a difficult time isolating the feeling from the story. Once they do, they notice the subtle tension of the feeling, and then reach the point of saying, "Warm and close," or "Closed and tight."

Interpretations:

An interpretation is what our Ego-mind "does" with the sensory (perception) and feeling data, all of which is influenced by our context. Interpretations are not true. They are explanations we create regarding our experience.

Possible ways of describing an Interpretation:

- "The story I am telling myself"
- "I judge"
- "I interpret"
- "I believe"
- "I think"
- "I assume"
- "I imagine"

Intention:

An intention is a clear statement that describes, "What I will do." It is also a re-statement of past promises, "It is my intention to always use the Communication Model, and so I will use it now."

Action:

What I actually do. Here is why I've made the Action box the same size as the other 5 combined: your intention is nice to know, but irrelevant. The only thing that matters is what you do.

The. Best. Relationship. Ever.

Example: This book will only work for you if you do as we suggest. Thinking about it and intending to follow the Tools won't change a thing. It's all about Action!!!

Reflection

This is your internal process of comparing what you said you would do (Intention) with what you actually did (Action). The two should match (integrity). You also evaluate the *result* of your behaviour. If your intention was to have a dialogue, and you use the Communication Model, and the discussion bogs down, the reflection process helps you to fine tune what you do next.

How to use the Communication Model

As we mentioned, the model can appear a bit kludgy. "Lots of words, not so sure why" kind of thing.

Like learning a foreign language, learning to communicate takes time and focus.

I'd like to encourage you to practice, even though it's going to seem a bit strange. Make a deal with your partner to take the time and effort to get each of the parts of the Communication Model listed above into the conversation. If you notice your partner missed one, invite him to add it. The task here is to practice doing this correctly.

The person listening does not respond to the information being conveyed! This is important. For example: "I see that your eyes are slightly closed and you have a line between them (Perception) and the story I am telling myself is that you are angry." (Interpretation)

This is not an invitation to debate whether you are angry or not. This is a practice session. And besides, even in a 'real' exchange, debating the *validity* of your partner's story is always a waste of time. So, just listen, and make sure all six of the areas we've discussed are covered.

Dialogue Examples

Example 1

- I see that your eyes are slightly closed and there is a line between them (perception)
- And I notice that my stomach is tight, and I'm clenching my hands, (feelings – internal states)
- and the story I am telling myself is that you are angry, (interpretation)
- and my past experiences in similar situations lead me to believe we're going to have a fight, (context)
- and I want to run and hide, but instead I want to check in with you (intention)
- so I'm staying put and asking you, "What's up for you right now?" (action – curiosity)

Example 2

- I make myself uncomfortable talking about sex (context)
- and I want to share with you what I'm experiencing (intention)
- and I notice that when I asked you about what you wanted sexually, you crossed your arms across your chest and crossed your legs (perception)
- and I felt cold and distant from you (feelings)
- and I judged that you were embarrassed and didn't want to discuss it (interpretations)
- but I really am curious, so I wonder if you'd like to explore what just happened? (action – curiosity)

The. Best. Relationship. Ever.

Example 3

- I'm noticing that you are looking at many of the women you're passing, and you even turned right around, (perception)
- and I have a history of making myself uncomfortable around not being the centre of a man's attention, (context)
- as my story is that every man I've ever been with has left me for another woman, and that you looking at women is, for me, a sign you're going to leave me. (interpretation)
- My body is shaking, and my chest hurts, and my stomach is upset. (feelings)
- I want to pick a fight with you and force you to pay attention only to me, but I know that that's what I used to do, and it got me nowhere, so... (intention)
- Let's sit and talk about my insecurities, and I'll explain how I'm feeling, and then invite you to tell me more about what you find attractive and a turn on, as I'm really curious about you, and working on getting over myself. (action)

The key to Elegant, Intimate Relating is the acceptance that every single thing that's going on for you is created by you – with the possible exception of your perceptions (but even then you're labelling what you see, etc. so it's still about you.)

The Communication Model is a way to take total responsibility for your side of your life, your experience. And then you share what you are figuring out with another, who is also curious about you.

Chapter Nine: Being Curious – and NODing

It seems to me that no matter how good I get at interacting and relating with Darbella, I am always practicing! The real issue is what happens when I lose focus and "slip."

A minor example:

Dar and I go to a yoga studio that has classes several times a week. A few years ago, I chose to annoy myself over my judgements about a classmate. So, as an experiment, we shifted to another night. I had a good time with the people at the new class.

Driving home with Darbella, I started into a bit of a rant about how I liked the class we'd just attended, and how much I disliked the regular one. Dar, when she could get a word in edgewise, said that the new class was OK, that she had no trouble with our regular class, and that I should decide which class I wanted to attend.

I wanted Darbella to join me in my drama, so I worked at getting her to agree that the old class was bad, weird, etc. and to agree that the new class was much better.

Dar repeated that either class was fine, and that this was my issue, and that I needed to make up my mind.

The. Best. Relationship. Ever.

I really wanted her to agree with me. I wanted her to join me in judging the person in our regular class. I tried everything. She refused to bite, and repeated that I had to decide about which class, as it was my issue.

I pouted and groused all the way home. Dar listened to my grousing and complaining, and did not try to extract me from my own mess. (Hint: she can't, as it's my issue. If she was silly enough to try, then I could judge that she'd not done it 'right.')

I created feelings of isolation and annoyance ("cold and distant,") then created the following interpretation: "You don't love me – no one does" – a personal favourite – and I just barely avoided saying, "I always support you, and you never support me." (I thought it, but didn't say it.)

Dar just sat there, repeating the mantra, "Your issue, you decide."

After 30 minutes, I got over myself, and calmed myself down.

Let me unpack this, as a way of describing Elegant, Intimate Relating

Thoughts on Superficial vs. Real Issues

Because our minds prefer complexity, we resist the idea that the 'many, many' issues we think we have are the same issue, in different guises.

Why? If I can convince myself that I have many problems, I can pretend I have too many to change.

One way of saying this is, "Baskin Robbins has 31 flavours (superficial issues,) and they are all ice cream (real issue.)"

Being Curious - NODing

- *Superficial* issues are easier to talk about.
- *Superficial* issues involve copious use of "you" and "he / she / they" – the "guilty party" is anyone but me.
- *Superficial* issues are described in either generalities or universals. ("He always (universal) does what I don't like (generality.)"
- *Real* issues, which are ongoing until we die, are the underlying cause. Typically, we have one or two real issues that we don't talk about – we'd rather focus on the superficial.

My **superficial** *issue* was which class to attend. I mean, really, all I had to do was get over myself and pick one or the other. It's a superficial issue that Dar was wise not to bite on.

My real issue is what's actually going on for me in the Here and Now

My **real issue** was (and continues to be) "winding myself up" – my internal processes colliding and building up a huge drama.

My **real issue** is that I wind myself up, and then blame my internal "winding" on the behaviour of others – I endlessly choose to create a sense of dis–satisfaction, as in "never satisfied."

As I didn't want to discuss the real issue, ("Boy, am I ever winding myself up right now! And I'm blaming my internal experience on the behaviour of others!") I attempted to draw Dar into my game. I desperately wanted Dar to agree that my arrogant judgements about the guy were **right**. Dar did not bite on this, and kept reminding me to examine my process of winding myself up.

Now, you might ask, what would have been the downside of Darbella joining me in a "right / wrong" diatribe?

The. Best. Relationship. Ever.

- If she joined in with and agreed with my judgements, we'd have created a bitch-fest of monumental proportions. I trust you have noticed that griping about how awful others are changes nothing. We could have agreed to do this, (and occasionally do!) and could have had fun being sanctimonious, but again, this accomplishes nothing.
- Dar also could have argued against my story about the old yoga class – and the fight would have been about something out of our control – the behaviour of the guy in our yoga class.

Additionally, I would have been fighting *with Darbella* over a superficial, external issue (the person in the class,) while hotly denying the real issue – the drama I was creating. And then, I could have blamed Dar for all of it!

Darbella chose the path of curiosity, presence, and "I" language

She separated my stuff from her stuff, and refused to shift focus – she kept redirecting my attention to the drama I was creating. She did this through her use of:

"I" Language: She clearly stated that she had no issues with the old class, was OK with the new class, and that she had no judgements about the participants.

Presence: Darbella only talked about what I was doing in the moment – what I was saying and doing in the car – how I was choosing to upset myself. She would not shift over to my preferred topic – my judgements about the past behaviour of the guy in the original class.

Curiosity: She asked me if I was aware of what I was creating, and if I was interested in dropping the drama. She reminded me that the drama and energy was all mine, and encouraged me to deal with the drama I was creating.

• • •

Being Curious - NODing

In the 30 minutes I chose to take before getting over myself, I tried all kinds of clever strategies to draw Dar into my game. She chose not to go there. Part of me was proud of her, and the other part was annoyed that she was so good at avoiding my games.

Let me make some suggestions

Your job is to notice how, when, and what you are creating emotions over. The only way to engage in Elegant, Intimate Relating is to take responsibility for you.

Your other job is to be open and curious about your partner. This is simple when there is no drama. You have to remind yourself to practice curiosity when you're knee-deep in drama.

When your partner becomes emotional, biting on their drama is never helpful. Your job is to be curious and neutral.

You calm yourself, then invite your partner to explore their real issue, and you do this using three concepts – **Notice, Own,** and **Decide**.

In other words, NOD

- Keep reminding your **partner** to **Notice** what is up for them, to **Own** their drama, and to **Decide** what they want to do next. I hope you're NODing right now!
- And you're also doing the **same for yourself**. NOD if you agree.

Noticing

Once you stop creating drama over superficial issues, and "really notice," you generally discover the real issue you are upsetting yourself over.

The. Best. Relationship. Ever.

In our illustration, I was stuck on my stories about the person in the old class, and stuck on Dar not agreeing with me. What I wasn't noticing was how I was winding myself up in the present moment (in the car) over stuff out of my control (the behaviour of others, which happened in the past.)

I was focussing outward, and then building internal stories to match my judgements, without noticing that I was playing a game of, "It's all their fault!"

Dar kept asking me to step back from my drama, and to notice that I was ramping myself up – that I was building up emotion, telling stories, and creating drama. And then, she invited me to notice that I expected her to agree that my drama was not only true, but the *only* way to view the situation.

Because we've been communicating with each other forever, we use shorthand: "Or, you could get over yourself." The longhand version (which you should use for a while) is,

"So, I'm noticing that you are winding yourself up over the story you are telling, and I'm curious if you need to do more of that, or whether you'd like to drop the story, and start exploring ways to work through the issue you're creating."

Owning

These three things really do occur in order. Owning requires that I first notice what I'm constructing. Once I notice, it is essential that I claim responsibility: "Wow. Am I ever winding myself up with all my story-making and justifications. I'm trying to control everything, except me!"

Most people want to skip this step, as it's altogether too much like admitting you're wrong. Or guilty. Yet, skipping it is tantamount to pretending that "the devil made me do it."

• • •

Being Curious - NODing

When you go off on a tangent, that's you, 100% you, going off on a tangent. It does not matter if you are correct. Even if the other person is a jerk, and you could actually prove it, so what? At the end of the day, what you can do is decide how you will act, in response to each situation.

So, you own your game. You first claim responsibility to yourself, then admit to your partner that you've gotten hooked into drama-making. No excuses, no justifications, and no dissembling – you just state what's really going on... for you.

"Wow. I was really off in my head, telling stories, blaming [others, you] for how I was feeling. As I let go of the story, I notice I'm right back into my real issue [making myself miserable, feeling hard done by, etc.] I think I need to [do something - yell, scream, etc.] and then, if you're willing, I'd like to come back to where this started and find a solution."

Deciding

Once you turn down the volume and the drama, all that remains is a decision. "Given the game I'm playing, what will I do next?" Like with the Communication Model, the most important ingredient is Action.

Back to the example: Dar was willing to attend either class, and was firm in pointing out that this was my issue. After the 30 minute drama, I decided to shift to the new class.

"OK. I get it. I need to decide what to do next, while I acknowledge the drama I created. [Here is what I have decided to do.]"

Now, occasionally, you're going to slip, *and both you and your partner* are going to bite on an issue. Again, it's **Notice, Own, and Decide**. You do this by paying attention to your

The. Best. Relationship. Ever.

own reactions. Tightness, anger, wanting distance – all are clues you're winding yourself up.

As soon as you Notice the argument you're in, stop fighting! Take **Own**ership of your side ("Man, was I ever winding myself up! I apologise. Let's figure out what's up for each of us, and talk about what to do differently.") and then **Decide** to act purposefully by shifting into the Communication Model.

Don't wait for your partner to do something. Act as soon as you notice you're winding yourself up.

Bonus example:

*So, I **notice** that I'm really distracting myself and not listening to you. I know (**own**) that this is an issue for me, and often happens when I'm thinking I'm not being heard, or I think I'm being ignored. I then pull away and shut down. I've **decided** to call myself on this, and let you know what I'm doing, and now I'm ready to listen to you.*

Chapter Ten: Letting go of Drama and Storytelling

The Danger of Drama

I am on a campaign to do away with what I call "mindless drama." Drama is a mental creation akin to a snow squall – you cannot see anything clearly – except that with drama, you are snowing yourself.

People create mindless drama because they are addicted to their feelings, their pain, their stories, or their dysfunction – yet have difficulty accepting that the drama is 100% internal and self-created.

This is a key issue – what you think is going on is a story – a drama – and there's nothing true about it, unless you make it "true."

This is why all of the examples in this book seem silly and superficial to you. You read them and say, "How could anyone get upset about that!"

And then, when you share one of your drama-stories, you're surprised (and angry!) when your partner "doesn't get it," and won't agree with you and shift behaviour.

You think you are being betrayed because your partner fails to behave according to your dramatic desires

The. Best. Relationship. Ever.

Initially, it seems obvious to my clients that any rational person would understand their demands, and would cooperate with them. After all, they ask, "Isn't what I am asking a 'little' thing?"

The problem is, the 'little things' are never-ending

The real issue is their insistence that what they imagine in their heads must be accepted by their partner as "real and true," and that love requires obedience.

Now, drama per se is not a 'bad' thing. There is nothing wrong with choosing to build a drama for myself. I can then milk it for all that it is worth – this is a part of being human.

As long as I acknowledge that my drama is a self-created choice, I can create it, and fully experience it without judgement, and without blaming my partner.

Drama only becomes a problem when we think it is either 'real' or 'true'

Drama is an internal, chosen behaviour and perspective. When we pretend that our drama is 'real,' we are living at the opposite pole from being present.

Dropping Your Stories, and Retiring the Drama Queen

Dropping stories and drama requires accepting that not much of life is aimed directly "at" me. Most of life happens without my noticing. This is another way of saying that the only things that are significant in my life are the things I notice.

If my story is that my life is miserable, I'll look for things I judge prove that I'm hard done by. If my story is that I only receive poor treatment, I'll be an expert in ignoring anything else – all I see is "I'm being treated poorly."

Letting go of Drama & Storytelling

Couples caught in story-telling and drama never get around to making choices

They forget that the intention of dialogue and relating is to create personal depth and meaning. They are lost in the story, and miss the obvious.

We get past this by actually listening to ourselves

One client is working on her B.A. She has an "A" average. One day, she was quite upset over an impending exam. She had convinced herself that she couldn't pass the exam.

Then, she said, "I suck at taking exams."

I replied, "You have an "A" average, so that means you've always gotten an "A" on exams."

She countered, voice trembling, "Well, I suck at exam preparation!"

Me: "You have an "A" average, so clearly your past exam prep has been great."

She sighed, and tried, "You just don't understand."

I countered, "Maybe you might just look at the truth of your "A" average, buckle down, stop complaining, and study for the exam."

Clearly, her stories of failure and hopelessness had no basis in fact. The issue was her "failure story," compounded by drama: "Not only will I fail the exam, but I'll get tossed out of University and end up living under a bridge!"

She'd worked so hard on the story that reality was meaningless. I spelled out reality to her, repeatedly, until she stopped telling negative stories. Then, we did some Bodywork to get rid of leftover feelings, and she went home to study.

The. Best. Relationship. Ever.

Our stories are created by our Egos to keep us stuck and "in line"

You will always tell catastrophe stories – always blame your partner – always look for problems where there are none. Your Ego keeps the stories going so that you'll think you are helpless, and will not rock the boat by changing anything.

We can't "stop" the stories, but we can notice them for what they are, acknowledge them, and let them go. We do this by learning to pay attention to our internal stories (not just spout them on auto-pilot,) and especially by monitoring and controlling what we say. (see "The Gap.")

If you spend a month or so paying attention to yourself, you'll begin to hear the tone of voice of your complaints – the arrogance, or the whine, or the demands. The lectures.

Once you clearly hear this stuff, you get a sense of what others have been listening to for years. Once you clearly hear, you discover your "auditory clue," and you then use it to stop, to breathe, to shut up, and to come back into presence.

Hearing Yourself

Here's the assignment for this section:

- First, it's your job to get yourself under your own control. It's not the job of someone else to sort you out.
- Begin by practicing hearing your tone of voice when you are in story / drama mode.
- Then, once you have "heard yourself clearly," sit with your partner, and describe what you've discovered. (Hint: it likely won't be news to them!)

As you continue to do this, you shift from auto-pilot to presence

Letting go of Drama & Storytelling

Now, make a deal with your partner – you want him / her to "just listen" when you wind yourself up. To sit there, observe, and invite you to continue.

You do not want your partner to rescue you, fix you, stop you, or divert you. You just want to get whatever it is off your chest.

This is your partner, not biting.

And your partner makes the same arrangement with you.

Now, of course, it's best if you both aren't caught in drama at the same time, although this will happen occasionally. If it does, all that's required is that one of you notice what is happening, and shift out of personal drama to listening and inviting the other to finish.

Creating a "pay attention phrase"

Drama needs expression, and it needs to be let go of. It's your job to learn to quickly "hear" and express your drama, and then stop!

However, sometimes we wind ourselves up so much that a little help from our partner is necessary.

As I mentioned last chapter, if I am going on and on, Dar will say to me, "… or you could get over yourself." I designed that line, and asked Dar to use it when she'd heard enough. I also promised her, and this is key, that I wouldn't "blame her" or pick a fight with her, for using it.

So, each of you, set up a pay attention phrase

- "I'm noticing that you are winding yourself up, and I'm wondering how much longer you need to do that."
- "You seem agitated. What's really going on for you?"
- "You could choose to get over yourself."

The. Best. Relationship. Ever.

Or invent your own!

Agree that the phrase can be used to invite the phrase-creator to stop with the drama, and ground himself / herself.

To recap: Your partner agrees to listen, to encourage you to "get it all out," and then invites you to stop. No analysis. Just support.

And you choose to do the same for him or her.

Chapter Eleven: Being Flexible

We are all masters of illusion. In order to understand the basis for living life in the freedom and clarity of Elegant, Intimate Relating, you have to choose to pay close attention to the games you play. Most people find this task daunting, but you can't be flexible if you refuse to pay attention.

The Dance of Co-Creativity

I was having quite the conversation with a client the other night. He's freshly out of a relationship and trying to figure out what happened. He was describing a typical conversation, and how the conversation would slide into a power struggle over who was 'right.' I mentioned several layers that are contained in any one conversation, and his eyes began to glaze over. He finally said, "I never knew it was so complicated."

Dar and I discussed this one morning, over coffee. We began by thinking about the different approaches to life and communication that we use – and that are used by people we know. We noticed several layers within any one exchange, and were only stopped by the clock.

I'm going to try to be as simple as I can be here, so bear with me. Each action we perform, each communication we have, has within it many elements. Here is a list of some of them.

The. Best. Relationship. Ever.

Self-responsibility – I am solely responsible for what I do – how I respond – to anything and everything that happens.

Freedom – I have the ability to do pretty much whatever I want to do.

Consequences – Each action creates an actual, yet "non-predictable" result.

Desired Outcome or Intent – Beneath every action I perform is my hoped-for result.

I could extend this list forever, but let's start here.

Self-responsibility

One of the main themes of this book is self-responsibility. It's an interesting perspective. My usage never varies – I, and I alone, create my experience. I interpret, I judge, and I create my emotions. It does me no good, and I am in error, to think that anything that goes on inside of me is caused by, or is the responsibility of anyone other than me.

The vast majority of people believe the opposite – that what "happens to them" is caused by others, by their upbringing, whatever. Listen to 100 people. See how many of them use blaming language: "He made me sad," or "She is making me cry," or whatever, instead of "I'm choosing to be mad about that," or "I am saddening myself."

You'd be hard pressed to find five people who talk in the second way.

For those who decide to become self-responsible, the work is endless. The interesting part is finding the balance between self-responsibility and sensitivity to the other person.

Freedom

Along with drawing breath, we all have an absolute right – a freedom – to choose to behave however we like. The more self-responsible we become, the more the "pull" to focus only on your own issues and perspectives. It takes great maturity to "hold on" to self-responsibility while considering your partner.

Let's say, for the purposes of this example, that you begin a freedom project. You decide to do or say whatever comes into your mind. You're doing this to experiment with a new way of being. So far, all well and good. Now, let's add in another person.

Consequences

Each action has a result, or consequence, attached to it. It is impossible to imagine a consequence-less action! Let's assume that I say x to my partner. My partner, upon hearing my words, does her "thing" – she interprets my words, and replies with y. Thus, the consequence of x, in this case, is y.

Many people get confused here. Because of self-responsibility, it's easy to act, and then ignore the reaction of my partner.

If I only focus on myself, then I do x, and do not care what y looks like

Let's imagine that my partner burst into tears, then got extremely angry, then left the room.

If *all* I am concerned with is my freedom, I might think, "I have the right to say whatever I want, however I want to say it. She needs to get over herself."

This is true, but not helpful. We need one more element:

The. Best. Relationship. Ever.

Desired Outcome or Intent

When *freedom* conflicts with *consequence*, the way past this is to remember your *intent* (see: Speaking Clearly.)

We're suggesting that the intent is "Having **The. Best. Relationship. Ever.** through Elegant, Intimate Relating."

Once I establish my intent, I endlessly observe the effect (result, consequence) of the choices I make and actions I perform, in relationship to my intent. I then choose my next action on the basis of my intent. It's really that simple.

I still have the freedom to say and do what I will

What changes is that I am now examining my behaviour through the lens of my intent. I include my partner's response as a key factor in determining my free choice of behaviour. Because of my intent, I become wiser and more observant as I act.

Let's go back to x and y. With the above intent in mind, I do or say x. I notice that my partner bursts into tears, gets extremely angry, and leaves the room. At this point, I have a choice.

I can get all righteous and say, "Her behaviour and response is her problem." And that would be so. My partner has chosen to have the reaction she had, out of all possible reactions. It is totally her responsibility to learn to bring herself under her own control.

However, and it's a big however, there is another choice

I can choose to remember that my intent is to deepen my intimate relationship with my partner. I therefore look at her response to my action or words, and I ask myself a simple question:

"Did my words [actions] get me closer to or farther from my intent to deepen my relationship?"

As soon as I ask this question, I am reminded that the ultimate freedom is the freedom to choose to act from a place of loving intent

Darbella and I have been caught in major disagreements. I'm remembering 3 or 4 times since 1984. We've had minor bumps in the road too – and worked through them by owning our own silliness, and returning to a place of re-establishing contact.

In the major battles, we've had the sense to briefly step away from each other, and in that space, to calm and soothe ourselves – to give ourselves time to get ourselves back to a useful way of relating.

We seem to know when "one more word" is going to toss us into some abyss

I certainly remember touching the "edge of the abyss" during the first major conflict we ever had, back in 1984. We were on our first long holiday, camping in Nova Scotia. Neither of us can remember what the fight was about, but we got to the "loud and angry point," went back to the campground, and I declared, "I'm putting you on a plane back to Toronto. I've had enough." I stormed off to the tent, while Dar sat on the picnic table.

I remember being furious, blaming Dar for the fight. I remember thinking, "I've had it. How dare she? Doesn't she know I'm a therapist? Doesn't she know how "together" I am? I'll show her!"

The. Best. Relationship. Ever.

In the midst of all of that, I somehow recognized the danger lurking "one more word" ahead. I buried my head in my sleeping bag and screamed a hundred or so obscenities. Then, I crawled out of the tent and asked Dar if she wanted to talk.

She did, I did, and we worked our way through whatever the issue was.

"Here I go, acting like an idiot. I'll stop myself right now." This is both simple and incredibly difficult. This is how to nurture Elegant, Intimate Relating.

Let's put it all together

Clearly, if my actions / words move me deeper into relationship, I will choose to repeat that behaviour. On the other hand, if my words or actions result in a disconnection between my partner and I, (and now, in addition to whatever x was, we'll have to work through her hurt, her anger and her walking out of the room,) I have a choice to make.

Many who think they get all of this, and judge that they are good communicators, none-the-less choose self-righteousness. "Phooey on this crap! I'll be damned if I'll change my 'self-responsible' behaviour just to make her happy! Besides, I can't make her happy. She's choosing this! Let her sit there in her misery! And the next time, I'll do it all over again!" Ouch.

If you choose to keep with your intent, you think: "Hmm. Interesting. I wonder how I can say or do that differently, right now. I can't control her choice of reactions, but I certainly can choose what I do. Rather than get defended and rigid, I can choose flexibility."

Being Flexible

Dar and I have been at this for years. We created our model, practiced it, refined it, taught it to others, and wrote books and articles about it. Does that make us experts?

Well, I'd say we're really, really, really good at EIR. And to an extent, we are experts at it. But we cannot allow our so-called expertise to turn into self-righteousness. Paradoxically, the more we choose flexibility, the less expert we become. In Zen, wise students are always "beginners!")

We continue to get 'better' at being curious, self-responsible, and caring. Expertise and self-righteousness get trumped by constant and changing EIR.

Here's the point:

"I choose, in my freedom, to declare myself flexible. In my freedom, I act. I then pause, and reflect on my action. What were the consequences of my action? Did I move closer to or farther from my intent? From a position of self-responsibility (as opposed to self-righteousness,) what will I freely chose to do next?"

In the "Speaking Clearly" chapter, we called this Reflection

Within each transaction between intimates are multiple elements, interacting. Each action has a consequence, both for the actor and for the recipient. Each response can come from self-responsibility or from self-righteousness.

It simply isn't simple. But spending your life alone (even within a relationship), for me, is not a palatable choice.

Choose to exercise your freedom in relation to your intent. Every time.

The. Best. Relationship. Ever.

** HOWEVER...

 **Each action has CONSEQUENCES**

| **So...** I can act without thinking... | **Or...** I can weigh the consequences (the response) |

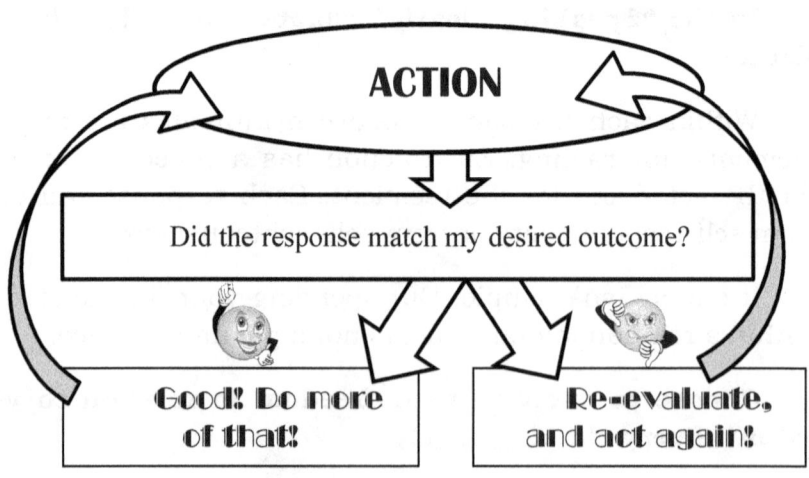

Chapter Twelve: Feeling Your Feelings

Let's remember Rule # 1 – what you feel, both bodily sensations and your emotional reactions, are yours. No one causes you to feel anything. This is a hard one to get, and tricky to live.

You and your partner need to remind each other of this. Then, you take it a step further, and come up with elegant ways to actually express your emotions.

Another hard one, especially as regards emotions considered 'negative,' or 'bad'

We have all kinds of excuses, theories, and prohibitions about expressing emotions like anger, grief, sadness, etc. We fear "falling into an emotion and never getting out." We fear witnessing strong emotions, of making ourselves scared, insecure and unhappy.

We also spend a lot of time denying our emotions

A couple spent the weekend with us, working, it turned out, on ending their relationship.

In the course of the weekend, the woman said that she never got "really" angry. She said she was "a little angry" with

The. Best. Relationship. Ever.

her dead dad, and also "a bit angry" with her soon-to-be ex-boyfriend.

During Bodywork, she *exploded* in anger – she screamed and thrashed, loudly, for 20 minutes.

After, she said, "Well. That was loud and surprising. But I never get angry, although I am still a little mad at my dad and my boyfriend."

Her actual experience – of great, loud, expressed anger – was instantly renamed "a little mad." She had taken her actual experience and chose to rename it "…a little mad."

Another, 'better' choice: to integrate the new data, expanding her self-definition – and she could have done this without judgement. Her new understanding, arising from the Bodywork experience, would have been," I hold much anger, and am able to let it go, loudly and safely."

Not right, not wrong, just new information

Early on, we are taught, by word and example, to create lists – some emotions are acceptable and some are not. I'll continue to use anger as an illustration, because lots of people have it on the 'bad' list.

When parents see their kids acting out anger, most force them to stop. They may try distraction, lectures, bribes, or one of the following brilliant sentences.

- "What have you got to be angry about?" Or,
- "I'll give you something to be angry about!"

It's not really about the kid's anger. It's about the parent. The parent is "bewitched, bothered, and bewildered" by their own anger. Not knowing how to safely express their anger, the parent becomes uncomfortable in the presence of the

Feeling Your Feelings

child's anger. Rather than "fix their own issue," they get the kid to stop.

At best, the child learns that emotions on the 'bad' list have to be justified before they can be expressed. And of course they learn they are never justified!

When we "get socialized," we become addicted to society's rules

Most people develop a socially acceptable, yet quite limited range of emotional expression. We grow up hearing that we have to justify what we are feeling, especially the emotions others judge to be messy, 'wrong,' or uncomfortable.

We have a minuscule range of expression, no words to describe their emotions, and a death grip on stuffing 'bad' feelings.

Time to check in

Have a look at how you are feeling right now. Tense? Doubtful? You may be scaring yourself: "Uncle Wayne is arguing for flinging 'bad' emotions all over the place!" And when you picture that, you go to your personal 'bad' list, visualize everyone running around screaming, and freak yourself out.

That's not what I'm suggesting

I'm suggesting that you examine your emotional 'good / bad' list, and discover what you're stuffing and avoiding dealing with. Then, you create ways to express your emotions safely.

There is no such thing as a safely stuffed emotion. Emotions build and build, and find their way out over the stupidest things. Much better, I think, to find a simple and efficient way to be our emotions. Briefly, and elegantly.

The. Best. Relationship. Ever.

Here are five ideas that will help. In the next section, the actual exercises!

1. Have a breath.

The reason we have to remind ourselves to breathe is that, when confronted with a 'negative' emotion, most people hold their breath. Breath holding is mostly a fear reaction. When we hold our breath, we lose our sense of Here and Now.

Breathing re-engages our presence. We come back into the present experience – as opposed to either checking out, (going numb) or fleeing into our heads and telling ourselves long-winded stories. One breath, followed by another and another, creates spaciousness and room for being present. (see on-line, for a video on Breathwork.)[1]

2. Have your emotions.

This is a favorite expression of my buddies Ben Wong and Jock McKeen, retired founders of The Haven. "Having" means that emotions are to be expressed – as opposed to being analyzed, justified, explained away, or repressed.

No matter how scary you make it to express "negative" emotions, as you become more emotionally mature, repression isn't an option. The cost in energy, passion, focus, and full bore living becomes a price you are unwilling to pay. (See the next section on how to express your emotions safely.)

---

[1] Here's the link to the bonus material:
http://www.phoenixcentrepress.com/the-best-relationship-ever/resources-for-the-best-relationship-ever/

3. Sit down and shut up.

Meditate, Meditate, Meditate! Learning to meditate helps us to see through our stories and to become present. There is no better approach to discovering yourself, observing your mind-games, and learning to let go of your judgements.

Meditation is all about noticing, and letting go.

Much of the letting go has to do with our thoughts. Minds go "yada yada yada," and then our Ego gets involved, and we think each "yada" is gold. Most of our thoughts reflect judgements that were implanted by our culture, and are meaningless.

The goal is **not** to stop yourself from thinking – that's not possible. The goal is to NOD – notice – thoughts come, thoughts go. Own that you will always think, but do not have to follow the thought – attaching to your thoughts, stories, or judgements is optional. Then do – let your attention shift from the thought to "just sitting."

So sit. Watch. Notice. Own. Do. And don't waste your time making a big drama out of it.

(Here's a link to a video I made, teaching basic meditation.) (see footnote 1 for link)

4. Get to know your body.

I say to clients, "Don't tell me what you're going to do – do it – let me see it. I only believe what you do, not what you say." (*Action* in the Communication Model.)

Many trust their minds, distrust their bodies, and hate what lies beneath the belt line – so many judgments about bodies, about sensation, about passion and sex.

The. Best. Relationship. Ever.

And yet, you are your body, you embody your emotions, your passions, your sexuality. You ignore this reality of your being at your peril.

Bodywork and Breathwork, massage, and the soft martial arts – tai chi, aikido, judo, and the like are ways to get into the body. You do these things in order to feel again.

Your body knows, and your body is speaking to you always. It's not always 'right,' but it is always available. It is one channel of knowledge and inspiration, worthy of much of your attention.

Look at your emotions, your stories about your emotions, and what you're attaching to. Have a breath, quiet yourself, and let go.

Ways to Express Emotions

Exercises and Stories

My friend, the late, great Joann Peterson, is remembered for her Haven course and book, called *"Anger, Boundaries and Safety."* The book is out of print, and used copies sell for ridiculous prices, so I'll mention here an exercise or two that she suggested, concerning emotional release.

Other suggestions come from my clinical practice, and from Bodywork.

Learning to Feel Your Feelings

We talked about feelings and interpretations in the Communication Model section. To recap, we feel things in the body, and the list of what we feel is short: hot / cold, close / distant, tight / loose, etc.

Feeling Your Feelings

Interpretations are the stories we tell ourselves about what we feel and what we observe (through our senses.) These things get confused, and for a reason. "Feeling" is a loaded word.

When we were kids, a parent likely said something like, "When you do that, you make me sad." What we thought was:

- we caused feelings, and
- playing the "feeling card" leads to guilt and compliance.

"Mom" played that card to guilt us into changing our behaviour, so she wouldn't have to deal with her own feelings! We bought it because we didn't know any better.

We toss the "feeling bomb" in an attempt to trick our partner into changing behaviours. It has become an ingrained habit, then, to call "everything" a feeling.

Our goal is to get both you and your partner on the same page, and that page is locating, owning, naming, and releasing your emotions.

Illustration

Me: "And what are you feeling right now?"

Client: "I'm feeling confused."

Me: "Confused is a thought, not a feeling. What are you actually feeling in your body?"

Client: (pause) "Tight, right here." (Pointing to stomach/solar plexus — home to self-esteem issues.)

Me: "Rub that spot, and breathe."

The. Best. Relationship. Ever.

Client: deep sighs, wet eyes, tears.

Me: "That's what you're feeling, right now. And that's you, expressing it."

Here's what to do:

- 1) Listen for your use of the word "feel," or "feeling."
- 2) If you are describing an actual physical sensation, (tight / loose, etc.) pat yourself on the back!
- 3) If not, correct your language: "Oops. That's an interpretation, not a feeling."
- 4) Locate the feeling in your body, and touch your body where you are feeling the feeling. "I am feeling tight in my stomach, and the story I am telling myself is that I am confused."
- 5) Rub the spot (or ask your partner to do it.) Keep breathing. Allow yourself to open up to the feeling.
- 6) Use one of the methods below to **express** the emotion.

Expressing Anger

Let's do the biggie first. Almost everyone has a visceral reaction to the anger of others, and a quixotic reaction to their own. Many, for example, justify their own angry outbursts, while condemning them in others.

The problem with expressed anger is that it is often directed at the other person, and thus seems scary

Let me be clear here. I am talking about expressing verbal anger, as well as pounding cushions, etc.

Physical anger (hitting, grabbing, slapping, etc.) directed at another is never OK!

We get over our fear of anger by creating a safe environment for expressing it. The person doing the expressing

Feeling Your Feelings

learns to express within safe limits, and the partner who is watching ups their tolerance for anger, loudly expressed.

In the following sections, we'll look at structures for safe expression of emotions. For now: emotions need boundaried expression. Using discussion prior to the expression, we establish "rules and tools" – this keeps the framework of safety around the emotional expression.

First, Here's a Story

When I was training to be a therapist, I led a group. All the participants were women, and all were cop's wives. The city had just disbanded the SWAT Team, the husbands were all pissed-off former members, and things were not going well for the wives. They decided to come in as a group.

One participant was a nurse, weighed about 90 pounds, and had a huge smile plastered on her face. (Nice teeth, as I remember...) I'd ask about her marriage, and she'd sigh and talk about his drinking, the fighting, him giving her the silent treatment. All the while, smiling and saying, "But it's OK. I keep doing what I can to make it better. It's not about me."

I was a bit green back then, so it took me about 4 sessions to shift things. I finally thought to ask her if she was angry.

"No! Of course not! He's having a hard time and taking it out on me, but it's fine! Really!" Beaming smile, bright teeth.

I picked up a 3' x 3' pillow. "Here. Imagine this is your husband. Try doing what your body needs to do."

Client: "Silly man! I'm happy! I'm fine."

I pushed her with the pillow. The smile faded a bit.

The. Best. Relationship. Ever.

>Client: "Don't."

>Me: (push, push) "Don't what? Aren't you just supposed to put up and shut up? (push, push)

>Client: "Don't!!"

A couple more pushes and she attacked the pillow I was holding, pounding and screaming. It went on for 20 minutes. She knocked me from one end of the room to the other and back again. My arms got so tired I put the pillow on the floor and sat next to her while she pounded on it. She calmed, smiled a real, small smile and asked for a hug.

I ran into her on the street 6 months later – she'd left the cop, and was doing really well without him. She also reported regularly pounding the crap out of her mattress.

Releasing Anger

>Ground rules:

- 1) **containment:** choose a physical location that is "safe" – a quiet location free from obstructions or "stuff." You could clear an 8' x 8' area rug (have a thick cushion available), or sit in front of a couch or chair with soft cushions, or kneel on your bed. The "area" you pick is the area you stay in.
- 2) **physical rules:** no breaking things. No touching living things with angry intent. Set a timer for 3-5 minutes.
- 3) **express the emotion:** use your mouth, your hands, perhaps your feet: for the time set on the timer, within the contained space, yell, scream, swear, pound a cushion. If you are lying on a pad or the bed, kick your feet.
- 4) **support from your partner:** while you can go off somewhere and do this by yourself, most of the time it's best if your partner is close at hand. This helps your partner to up his/her tolerance for witnessing anger.

- 5) **timing:** when the timer goes off, stop. Ask yourself if you need "more." If so, re-set the timer for another 3-5 minutes.

Anger Variation

Stomping out the anger is also effective. Follow the above rules 1 and 2. Establish a "course," perhaps around a room.

- 1) This one "needs" a partner. The angry person starts walking and stomping. With each stomp, say something, like "No!" or a swear word, of a short sentence. Loudly.
- 2) Your partner walks alongside, prompting: "You can stomp harder than that!" "Stomp harder!" "Keep it up! Let that go!"
- 3) Same time parameter, using a timer.

And Another – The pillow push

See the story above. This needs a 3 foot square, thick pillow. Invite the angry person to "personalize the pillow." In other words, picture the pillow as the person or situation (s)he is angry at. Using blame language is OK here! The goal is to get the anger out at the inanimate object, so do what you need to – ramp it up!

Pushing with a pillow works if the partner can "manage" the pillow and the size / strength of the angry person. If the angry person is substantially larger, or stronger, put the pillow on the floor, and feed sentences to the angry person.

If you can manage a few pushes, say the following: "Make this cushion the person / situation. I'm going to push you a bit. As your anger arises, I'll lower the pillow to the floor. Follow it down and pound the pillow."

The. Best. Relationship. Ever.

Lastly, Hand Pushing

Like the last one, size matters ;-)

If you and your partner are approximately the same size, try this:

- 1) set the timer for 3 - 5 minutes
- 1) define your space. Stand facing each other. Reach out with both hands, and press against your partner's palms, palm to palm.
- 3) push against each other. One partner says, "Yes!" While the other says, "No!" Push hard, but with control. The object is to get to a "hard push balance," not to win. Let the volume rise with the intensity of the push.
- 4) Other word possibilities: You will! / I won't! You have to / I don't have to You're wrong! / No, you are!

Figure one out that you use when fighting, and try it out.

Expressing Grief

There is a difference between sadness and grief.

Sadness: I like to think of sadness as the "background hum" of dis-satisfaction that all of us build up. The physical expression of sadness is crying.

Grief: is the reaction to deep personal loss (death, separation / divorce, loss of a job, betrayal, etc.) The sound of grief is deep, wracking sobbing.

Example: Darbella really liked her uncle. The night after he died, she woke up a 1 am, and wanted to talk. She told stories, cried, and I listened and handed her Kleenex.

She wound down. I thought, "There was the sadness, I wonder about the grief."

We have a deal that we are free to work on each other's bodies without asking each time, so I pressed my thumb into her sternum (see video on Bodywork points.) She sobbed and shook for 10 minutes. That was the grief part. The grief would not have gotten expressed without the extra "effort."

Sadness and grief are not things to "fix." Because both tend to trigger the observer's own pools of sadness and grief, we typically react by saying: "What can I do to make it better?" "It will get better with time."

This is, "Racing in, trying to cut off the emotional expression."

You're not going to do that anymore, right?

Ground rules:

- 1) when sad, or when in grief, **make yourself comfortable**. Climb into bed or onto a comfy couch. Partner, bring Kleenex, and a "waterproof shoulder."
- 2) **Partner, sit nearby**, but let the grieving person set the distance. Your job is to sit there, keep breathing, be available for hugs, and to pass Kleenex.
- 3) Breathe. **Feel into your body, and locate the sadness / grief.** Likely it will be in your chest, beneath your sternum (breast bone.) Place your fingers on the "sore spot," and press inward until you feel an aching pain. Also experiment with asking your partner to do this for you.
- 4) **Loosen:** Wiggle your jaw, and press inward on the jaw hinges – keep your jaw loose, and begin to sigh and let sound out. Return to pressing your sternum.
- 5) **Breathe** deeply into the pain, and really let the sound and tears out. Let your body shake, sob, cry – let your body go.

The. Best. Relationship. Ever.

Adding a cradling

The sad / grieving person can ask for, or be offered, a "cradle" while expressing the feeling.

Version 1) partner, sit next to the person, and put an arm around their shoulders. Recipient, wiggle in and make yourself comfortable.

Version 2) the sad person sits in the partner's lap, gets comfortable, cuddles in, and works through the emotion. It's even possible for the "cradler" to push the sternum point while holding and supporting the person with the other arm.

Be sure both of you are comfortable! The partner should be seated against a supportive surface, and both parties need to move around as the process continues, to maintain their own level of comfort.

EIR is really a dance. We reach out both to provide a comforting environment, and also to explore our own arising and emerging thoughts. As we witness the process of another, we are drawn more deeply into our own process. Because we are not running away or trying to "cut off" expression, our partner finds a safe place to work their issue through to completion.

This can also be done standing

Back when I was in the Ministry, the child of a young couple I quite liked died.

When I got to the house, there were lots of people in the room, all mouthing platitudes, "He's in a better place," "God's will," "You're young, you can have another," etc.

The couple was off to the side, sitting quietly and forlornly on the couch, obviously containing themselves so as not to upset their families. I got rid of the assembled masses, and said, "This sucks, my heart is breaking, and I'm right here."

I held out my arms, and they both rushed over to me. We hugged and cried on each other's shoulders for 15 minutes.

Other Emotions

Anything that you feel in your body can be explored. You'll see physical exercises for erotic and sensual feelings two chapters below, for example. The key is to "push into" your feelings, so as to feel them completely. In Bodywork, I say, "Breathe into that and make it bigger."

That's the direction to take! Express it, and let it go.

Finding Joy

Here's a simple exercise or two for really letting go, getting your heart pumping, and having fun with your partner.

Darbella and I were visiting friends, and the music was on quietly in the background. Suddenly, the volume got cranked up, and "*Jesus, Oh What a Wonderful Child*" by Mariah Carey was playing. She said, "We call this the Jumpin' Jesus Song!" Up she and her husband bolted, and soon they were jumping and bouncing around the living room. It was like aerobics to soul/gospel music.

Dar and I do something similar, sometimes, when we hug (no music necessary!) Right in the middle of the hug, one or the other of us holds on tight and starts hopping in a circle. The other person pretty much has to go along. Then we hop in the opposite direction, to "unwind!"

In both cases, everyone is bouncing about, and laughing. And the point of the exercise is to do so, for no apparent reason. You soon "get" that a deep pool of joy and happiness ex-

The. Best. Relationship. Ever.

ists in us, in our hearts, and it doesn't take much to kick it into gear.

More Practice in Feeling what you Feel

This little exercise opens us to how much sensory data is coming in, all the time. It explains the late 60s comment, "I dig your vibe!"

Our bodies do exude energy, and we pick up on (resonate with) the "feel" of the energy of others. We vibrate to their vibration, and this explains our feeling drawn (close) to some, repelled by others. Mostly, we don't listen to this "vibe," and lose out on interesting information.

Fortunately, if you have some willing friends, you can practice, and learn.

Exercise:

This can be done with as few as one other person, up to a small crowd. For purposes of explanation, I'll talk about working with one person. (Group directions below)

Pick a partner, stand about 10 feet apart. One person directs, the partner follows the director's hand motions. Hand motions are: come closer, stop, step away.

- 1. Director goes inside and feels for the other person's energy. Sounds odd, but we're picking this "vibe" up all the time. We're doing it subconsciously, and this exercise brings it to consciousness. Just "feel" for the person with your heart and belly. You'll feel something akin to a tingle, and you will notice how you feel about it. (wanting more / wanting less, attracted / repelled, warm (hot!) / cold, etc.)
- 2. Director, signal the partner to take a step forward, then signal stop. Director, feel the shift in energy. Repeat. Sig-

Feeling Your Feelings

nal partner to come closer. Partner, take one step and stop.
- 3. The partner can "feel" too, but should mostly just follow the hand directions. You can talk about what you are experiencing, or just have the experience quietly.
- 4. Repeat until the partner is close, or, trusting the "vibe" you feel, you might choose to signal the person to step aside. No words or explanations are given!

What happens with a group is:

- 1) the group members line up behind each other.
- 2) follow the above procedure.
- 3) when the first person is either waved off or makes contact, the "director" has a breath, clears their energy, and invites the next person forward with the hand signal.

This is an internal exercise of observing your feelings

Lots of times, the internal feeling shifts with distance, say from neutral, to uncomfortable (as the person crosses your "polite distance" boundary), to pleasant, to chargy.

It's good, then, as the person crosses your invisible "comfort boundary," (Too close!"), to have a breath and wait a second or two.

What might happen is that your boundary adjusts and opens, and you suddenly want the person closer. Had you closed down immediately, you would have sent the person packing.

This is how people who say they crave contact, yet never have any, react. They shut down too soon.

The opposite side of the coin is ignoring the "uncomfortable vibe" feeling, and bringing the person closer, so as not to

The. Best. Relationship. Ever.

"hurt their feelings." Many people do this – and end up with friends, lovers, partners they feel discomfort with.

This exercise is helpful for becoming really aware of the guidance your body is providing, all the time, and helps you to pay closer attention.

These are exercises in letting go

Go inside and ask yourself, "What am I afraid of?" "What am I resisting?"

Then, ask yourself, "What could I do, in the real world, to gain some experience with this?"

Be courageous! Set something up, with partners, friends, with your therapist. Just press a bit – discover what you are stopping yourself from feeling, have a breath, and go where you fear going (pound the pillow!) – see what releases.

Chapter Thirteen: Exploring Sensuality and Sexuality

The Essential Conversation

You might be wondering, "Why dialogue about sensuality and sexuality?" I would suggest that our sexual nature and our ability to be sensual (engage fully with our senses) is fundamental both to our human natures, and to our well-being.

This is an issue for many people – many of my clients squirm when I broach the topic. Some clients go so far as to cross their legs, and fold their arms over their chests, look away, and say, "Oh no. I'm fine with sex."

I tend to think not.

Sensuality and Sexuality are often mixed in with guilt and shame

We're not born that way. Young children experience their feelings directly, and "in the moment." That's why they can be having a tantrum one moment and giggling with pleasure the next.

They stop spontaneous expression as they learn to have judgements. They begin to question their experience, as op-

The. Best. Relationship. Ever.

posed to having it. "SHOULD I be feeling this way?" invariably leads to, "It's WRONG to feel this way!"

Learning to evaluate situations on a 'good / bad, right / wrong' scale is necessary for the child's survival (so, for example, they don't walk into the "pretty" campfire.)

It goes off the rails because of "societal confusion." Western society especially seems quite confused about matters sensual/sexual. First, sex sells. Second, sex is embarrassing when it's "me and mine."

Most adults have their own unresolved issues around sensuality and sexuality. This happens because sexuality and sensuality is thought of as a "thing to be done" as opposed to an aspect of who we are.

As children, we learn to distrust and repress our bodily sensations in favour of judgements, guilt, shame, and "over-thinking." We "get it" that sex is important, but also get that people in authority over us might get uncomfortable with it.

Yet, our sensuality and sexuality are a deep and hard wired part of us

We are born to feel, and feel deeply. The childhood days of ecstatic living seem to taper off and go background around school time, (the Latency Stage) only to re-surface with a vengeance at puberty – with a heightened sexual awareness.

All along, and increasing at puberty, there's societal pressure to behave – coupled with the adolescent's sense that their emerging sexual nature makes the adults around them uncomfortable. (I hear parents say, "I just want my little girl / boy back!")

Exploring Sensuality and Sexuality

Adolescents are drawn deeply to the charge of sexuality / sensuality, and are also confused or disturbed by the guilt and shame that arises.

Added to this, parents who discuss sexuality fully with their kids are rare. Clinical discussions happen and there might be STD / birth control discussions, but not much about fully feeling feelings, about elegantly expressed sexuality, etc.

So, just when the engines are firing on all cylinders, the teen is abandoned to figure it out for himself / herself.

Most of us first experimented with sex literally or figuratively in the back seat of a car. One or both participants were totally clueless, and what happened was awkward. These are called "grope sessions" for a reason – nobody seems to know what's going on, (groping in the dark) and the result was sloppy, dumb, and not much fun.

The milestones, the "firsts," are also inelegant. In 30 years, I only remember one or two clients who had a positive experience with "first intercourse," and that includes the males, who often mention feeling stressed, and "expected" to know what to do next.

One of my clients described her first sexual encounter as, "He grabbed me, groped me, had his way with me, and then said, "You're a lousy lover. You're likely frigid, and I never had these problems with other women." She was well aware of his issues, but also stopped having sex for two years.

Other clients have difficulty "relating" to their genitals. They don't like the way they look, judge the way they work, and in general find it difficult to talk about what they need and want. (see the exercises section.)

The. Best. Relationship. Ever.

Some clients became "hyper-sexualized." Yet, as they step back, they realize that their relationships are all "sex based," and intimacy is foreign to them. "I realized all (s)he wanted was sex."

If sexuality is not discussed, experienced through exercises, and practiced in depth, you'll stay "stuck in the back seat." More "groping around" is not enough – that would be like giving your teen the car keys and saying, "Go figure out how to be an excellent driver, all by yourself."

Most people never learn about sensuality

Many of my female clients bemoan their lack of "cuddling." They want sensual, or erotic, non-sexual contact, or perhaps a massage, and every time they try to get it, their partner thinks it's an invitation to sex. If they decline, their partner makes demands, gets angry, or gets up and leaves.

And then, there's frequency

Sexual frequency, desire, and "what I want" varies – person to person, by temperament, mood, age, and "life." Many couples seeking therapy are miles apart on "who wants to do what with whom, and how often." Pressure is exerted, or the "silent treatment" applied, as dialogue seems impossible.

By the time people get to therapy, their sensual and sex lives, in the main, are boring, shut down, predictable, and infrequent.

Without effort, we end up surrendering a part of our souls

There was a golden age of sensuality some centuries ago, which saw our sensual and sexual natures not only as fun, but as essential tools for spiritual and personal growth.

(Google: "sculptures at the Khajuraho Temple in India" for an example.)

The Hindu / Jain Khajuraho Temples were built over a span of 200 years, from 950 to 1150. They celebrated daily life, the progression of human understanding, and included erotic sculpture as one of the methods for enlightenment.

Sexuality was seen (through Tantra, for example,) as a way to deepen spirituality and come into a fuller and richer existence. Many paths, and sexuality was one of the gates.

This way of being got pushed background around the time of the Dark Ages, through the influence of Augustinian Christianity, Islam, (Islamic invaders desecrated the Temples,) and a more rigid Hinduism.

Religions have been particularly harsh regarding women. Women were (and in some cultures, still are) blamed for polluting the minds of men (like men need any help…)

Many religions "solved" this "problem" by literally and figuratively wrapping women up and sticking them on a shelf. Shaming and blaming women goes on and on.

To explore the sex-positive perspective, all you have to do is read the Song of Songs in the Bible, or study Tantra and Kundalini practices from India, or "The Jade Chamber" from China.

Our sensual and sexual natures are not optional

They are a part of us – a fairly big part, actually. We are turned on, physically and mentally (the brain being our largest sex organ.) The turn on begins at the cellular level, and extend to our "total bodies" and beyond.

The. Best. Relationship. Ever.

We are conditioned to go into "story-ville," – to block noticing what we are feeling – we push the charge down below our consciousness – we even deny our true nature – and thereby create a background sensation that "feels like a painful longing" for true contact – sound familiar?

To heal ourselves, our position regarding our personal level of sexuality and sensuality needs to be "re-formed."

The Khajuraho Temple in India points us in the right direction. The temple sculptures demonstrate how sensuality, sexuality, and spirituality are entwined. Given the positions demonstrated by some of the statues, "entwined" is a great choice of words. ;-)

This golden age was a time of experimentation – and the experimentation involved using yoga, massage, meditation and Tantra – physical techniques designed to open participants to the free movement of energy in the body.[1]

People learned to use pleasurable sensations and sensual / sexual activity to build up, strengthen, and move the energy up the spine, to the top of the head, and back down, in order to open to a deeper, energetic way of being. (see Exercises.)

Sensuality and sexuality are elegant methods for deepening one's self-knowing, and in that process, opening yourself both to bliss and to a more intimate relationship with your partner and others.

Or, as Joseph Campbell put it,

---

[1] I could have just written Kundalini energy, but am choosing, in this book, to stick mostly to Western descriptions. Some of the exercises in the next section come from yoga, Tantra, and Kundalini work, but again, I'll describe it without very much "Eastern language."

Exploring Sensuality and Sexuality

"If you follow your bliss, you put yourself on a kind of track that has been there all the while, waiting for you, and the life that you ought to be living is the one you are living. When you can see that, you begin to meet people who are in your field of bliss, and they open doors to you. I say, follow your bliss and don't be afraid, and doors will open where you didn't know they were going to be." ~ Joseph Campbell Quote from "A Joseph Campbell Companion"

Here's the point. Your sensual and sexual nature is real. It is fundamental to who you are

Yet, clients complain that their life is not stimulating, fun, inspired, passionate and creative. Most just put up with this. Many are the people who have had 'bad' sensual / sexual experiences and "stay stuck there," refusing to move past the accumulated pain, judgment, and distress.

Because of this, working with these feelings can initially be uncomfortable. If you breathe into your discomfort, you'll learn to accept these feelings as a part of you. Then, using Bodywork and the exercises in this book, you'll bring yourself to greater wholeness.

Sensual experience is not a head experience

You'll not find a satisfactory *explanation* for why it is essential that we feel, and feel deeply. (see "Feeling Your Feelings.") Rather, you surrender into the feelings, and surrender of the need to know "why."

In order for this to become real, you need to work on your sensual / sexual self

We do this, as we relax, play, explore, study, and experiment. Not to "prove" something, but to re-engage with this area of ourselves.

The. Best. Relationship. Ever.

There's nothing magical about sex, but it is powerful!

Our bodies are complex, and often ignored. What's missing is interplay between genitals, heart, and mind.

- It's your "heart energy" that creates intimacy with another.
- Our minds, with training, can learn to focus on making choices that build, rather than divide.
- What's missing? Cultivating a "genital-based" energy – through direct erotic exploration.

Vulnerability Projects

I encourage my clients to create Vulnerability Projects to explore being open and honest with another person. This open exploration might also include some erotic / sexual exploration.

The process begins when someone wants to explore something / practice something. Let's say it's communication, using the Communication Model. (see "Speaking Clearly")

The agreement would be to meet for 20 minutes to an hour per day and use the model while talking, and all of this is flexible and re-negotiable.

Thus:

"I am interested in exploring the Communication Model with you, and I'd like to set up a Vulnerability Project. I'd like to meet you from 1 – 2 and to practice. I want to talk about who I am and what I'm discovering about myself, and I'd invite you to do the same. Are you interested in doing this with me?"

Erotic Vulnerability Projects

This is an expansion on a standard Vulnerability Project. It's an opportunity to explore interesting or difficult physical activities / sensations. As I said earlier, most adults are reluctant to talk through sensual and sexual issues – this "Project" is a framework for doing so.

You want to be clear about the framework. A boundary could be "where on the body" – contact above the waist only, or "hugging and kissing only," or "massage everything except the genitals."

It could be an exploration of an "issue," such as difficulty with orgasm, premature ejaculation, etc., or a variety of sexual expression.

You might create an Erotic Vulnerability Project to address the "cuddling" issue mentioned above:

"Let's set up an erotic massage project, (see exercises) take turns on two separate days, and set a limit: 'just hugging, no intercourse, afterward.'"

Establish an Erotic Vulnerability Project

This Project is about sexual / erotic exploration. The goal is to explore your erotic selves, to learn to move, harness, develop, and deepen the erotic energy in your bodies. It's also about establishing a framework to explore areas of curiosity, or techniques you might have found difficult in the past.

Erotic / Sexual Vulnerability Projects are a perfect way to practice asking for what you want. You have a safe setting to explore how things feel in your body.

The. Best. Relationship. Ever.

Thus:

"I am curious about my sexual and sensual / erotic desires and responses, and I'd like to create a Vulnerability Project to explore this. I also want to discuss my sexual attractions, my microdot, (see "A Beginner's Guide to Screwing Up") and how I will choose to engage with other people as regards physical contact.

I want to do exercises with you, designed to explore sensuality, and I want to practice massage, cuddling and touching for their own sake – not as a prelude to intercourse.

I want to explore our sex life, and come to an understanding about frequency, being open about making requests, setting limits, and discussing and teaching you what my turn-ons are.

I'd invite you to do the same. Are you interested in doing this with me?"

Dialogues about Sexuality

OK, first rule: The time to discuss sexual desires, performance issues, and attractions to others is "much before" or "well after" sex. Not in the middle of. Because almost everyone has deep issues around sex, performance, attractiveness, "during" is not the time to "complain, raise issues, or be critical."

Having this discussion "during" shifts us "into our heads" and away from the heart – this removes us from the shared experience with our partner.

As you discovered in "Speaking Clearly," good dialogue follows the Communication Model. So do Sexual Dialogues. Yet, this arena is one in which "dumb comments" prevail. This is due to our discomfort around discussing our sexual natures and desires, coupled with a tendency to turn sex into a battle.

Sally, she of the high libido, endlessly criticized Sam, and especially on the rare occasions they had sex. She kept up a monologue about his inadequacies, the 'much better' performance of her myriad of prior partners, and about how Sam must be dysfunctional to "not want more of this!"

Yikes. Sure. Hearing that, I imagine Sam can't wait to do it again.

So, save the comments for non-sexual dialogue time. Remember, this needs to be done with sensitivity and care, using the Communication Model.

However: asking for what you want, "during," is always OK! It's necessary.

Directions: "Down a bit and a little to the right."

Requests: How much pressure, how you want to be touched or held, what you want to experiment with.

Checking In: same questions as above: "How is the pressure," "How is this position or technique for you," "Is there something you'd like to try?"

Use of boundary words: "stop" words, or pacing words when exploring new things, can be used "in the middle of it."

Before or after times are for setting up Sexual Projects

This is also the time to let your partner know about your "patterns and habits." (see first example, below.) You also use this discussion time to set up new explorations, ask for feed-

The. Best. Relationship. Ever.

back or information, and let your partner know if something isn't working for you.

Let me give you a couple of examples of great Sexual Dialogues:

Healing: This story is an amalgam of two of my clients. "She" had traumatic past sexual experiences, and got teary / cried as she neared orgasm.

With other partners, she did what she could to "stuff" the sad feelings. She tightened up her body so as not to cry. Then she went into her head, and kept repeating, "Don't cry!"

Usually, she sobbed anyway, and turned her head away. The guy, confused and thinking he had "done something wrong," always pulled back and apologised. She'd mumble, "It's OK, it's not really you," and get out of bed.

Needless to say, the sex was not so hot.

I suggested the following, and in each case, the partner finally learned what was up, and what was wanted / needed. (This is an example of letting your partner know in advance something you know about yourself!)

"I want to talk about what happens for me sexually. I've noticed that I sometimes, during intercourse, I have moments of being really sad, and sometimes I cry during sex. I want you to know that this is about me. [You could tell the back-story here.] Nothing is broken, nothing needs fixing. I think I just need to get some "sexual tears" out. So please, just slow down a bit, make eye contact with me, hand me some Kleenex, and remind me to breathe. I'll make eye contact with you, and stay in my body, and continue making love."

• • •

Exploring Sensuality and Sexuality

Both discovered that making eye contact and "keeping on going" led, in short order, to the tears no longer occurring. This is an example of Sexual Healing.

Experimentation: You likely have positions, variations, or fantasies that you'd like to explore. Springing such wishes on your partner "during" might work (with luck!) We suggest a "before or after" conversation to discuss what you want and how to proceed (if your partner is willing.)

This also means that whatever "material" you need, (props, lube, etc.) is close at hand. Nothing kills the mood quicker than, "Hold that thought! I'll be right back! I forgot to buy a flyswatter!" rotfl

"I want to explore [this variety of sexual expression.] I'd like to take it slowly, and want you to go slowly too. I'm going to use "green" as a slow-down word, and "pineapple" as a stop word, and I'll say it if things get too intense for me. I'd then like you to either slow down or stop, but maintain physical and eye contact. Are you interested, and will that work for you?"

Sexual Issues: Sexual issues do happen. Because our sexuality is interwoven with our being, what affects our bodies and / or minds effects our "genitals" – our sexual desire and performance.

Nothing "cools our jets" like a good dose of stress, hardship, a "death" (death in the family, loss of job, etc.) or conflict. Age plays a factor too.

Other issues might come from our sexual history, (such as the "crying" story, above) and might result in issues like low or non-existent desire / orgasm, premature ejaculation, painful intercourse, etc.

The. Best. Relationship. Ever.

The most interesting work in this arena is called sensate focus. We use non-reciprocal sensate experiences and focussed touch to help our clients to let go, stop judging themselves, and to experience.

Here's how to set that up with your partner:

"I'm having difficulty with [orgasms, premature ejaculation, etc.] and I want to explore what's up. I'd like to set up a Vulnerability Project where we talk about my experiences, do some research, (talk to a therapist) and then practice some exercises that might help me to work through this. I'd like to ask for 2 times a week to do the exercises, and also time to debrief after. How is that for you?"

About Attraction and Physical Contact with Others

This happens to each of us, although many might pretend it doesn't. So, tackle the topic early and often, and come to an agreement each time!

All of us become emotionally interested / attracted to others, and sexually attracted to some. We talked about this in the Microdots section.

Denying this, or trying to repress it, is deadly.

Many years ago, I worked briefly with a woman who had been engaged before, and she'd ended the relationship after her fiancé "cheated on her." She described a dating history of exactly the same thing – dating, cheating, and dumping.

Now, she was getting married, and she was convinced he'd eventually cheat on her too.

Her: "I watch him like a hawk. He's always checking out the waitresses asses, and ogling women in the super-market. He talks to his secretary all the time. I'm constantly digging my elbow into his ribs, and telling him to pay attention only to me!"

Me: "How's that working?"

Her: "He says he understands, but then he looks at the next woman who walks by."

Me: "Do you ever check out cute guys?"

Her: "What? Me? (blushing scarlet...) Well... yes, all the time, but that doesn't matter, because I'd never cheat."

Me: "Do you think that you have one set of rules for yourself, and another set for him? And do you think that your focus on cheating is going to help?"

Her: "Well, I have to do something, because every relationship I have ever been in has ended in cheating, no matter how loudly I demanded that they only focus on me."

And on and on, and around we went, and she ended therapy. I then occasionally met with her husband. He reported that she continued to focus on what she saw as her husband's wandering eye.

The relationship suffered, and communication almost stopped, except about, (you guessed it!) him and his 'problem.' Eventually, she "caught him" having dinner with a female friend. She thought she was right again!

Except she wasn't.

I think it's silly to expect Darbella to only have me as the "male person" in her life, and vice versa. We definitely find others attractive, and some sexually attractive. (a microdot.)

We decided what to do about this very normal phenomenon at the beginning of our relationship (way back in 1983.) We made an honesty pact (see: "Total Honesty"), and quite intentionally include sexual attraction as a "reportable" item.

The. Best. Relationship. Ever.

Dar knows my microdot, and I know hers.

Dar's not jealous of my "attractions," and I'm not jealous of hers. Our "boundary" around relating with others is "honest reporting, not repressing."

Discussing Attraction / Microdots

In *"This Endless Moment,"* I suggested going to the beach, sitting with your partner, and both of you telling your partner which people you find attractive, and which ones (far fewer) are your microdot. You will, if you let yourself, cease to be uncomfortable talking about what you find attractive, or hearing about the same from your partner.

Here are the necessary dialogues:

1) attractions

Form an agreement to let your partner know, ASAP, when you find someone attractive[2]. If you meet someone, and decide s/he is "friend-worthy," you let your partner know.

Let me be clear: we inform our partner because we are committed to total honesty, not because we're looking for permission! Because there are no secrets, and because we have agreed on boundaries, the consequence is: new, interesting input for future dialogue.

The only betrayal, in this regard, is dishonesty. Now, I know. Telling your partner seems scary, and there's some kind of rush that comes from sneaking around.

---

[2] And by attractive, I mean interesting, or "of note." In other words, if I can come up with some reason for NOT talking about my relationship with someone, I need to get over myself and talk about it with my partner. No secrets, including secret relationships.

Dishonesty, however, will always come back to bite you in the butt.

This is why we suggest talking this through in advance of needing to. Because, as you likely know, getting "found out" is a whole lot more complicated than being honest from the start.

So, decide: That the gist of all conversations with others will be shared with your partner – that you will or won't share conversations with your principal partner with others. Lay it all out.

"I expect that I will continue to meet people of the opposite sex that I find attractive. I will always let you know who the person is, the context of our relationship, [at work, at the gym, etc. – the Content from the Communication Model,] and what my Intention is." (see below)

2) physical contact

Given the Workshops and Residentials we lead, and the Bodywork we do, making physical contact with others is a given. That said, in our "civilian" life, we follow the above pattern – boundaries are established in advance, and we report in honestly as contact is made.

Because our only "rule in the sand" is Total Honesty, (see "Total Honesty") we have engaged in Physical Vulnerability Projects with others. We've established quite flexible rules and boundaries for exploring touch, physical and sexual contact, etc.

That's just us, and we're not "selling" that position.

We *are* "selling" endless dialogue about what turns you on, who you are attracted to, and what the boundaries are regarding physical contact.

The. Best. Relationship. Ever.

What we have chosen may not "work" for you, but **not** talking about "attractions to others" with an open mind likely will lead to an unpleasant surprise down the road.

So, talk it through. You might decide, initially, that hugs or hand-holding with non-partners is OK. That going for tea is OK, but kissing on the mouth isn't. That there's a "boundary" at the waist. Whatever.

What is essential is:

- 1) a preliminary discussion, and an agreement, and
- 2) a continual discussion, especially if either of you decide you want to "loosen" the parameters. (Hint: one or the other of you, or both, as time goes by, will want to.)

"Here is what I propose as physical boundaries with others. [Think about this carefully, and write it down. Have your partner do the same. Compare, talk through, and reach 100% consensus."]

3) erotic / sexual contact

Short paragraph. Again, I have no "rules" for you here. In my relationship, the only rule is "total honesty."

That said, you need to determine what's best for you as a couple, and as above, keep exploring the "set-point."

My sense is that open, honest, vulnerable exploration is key to personal growth, and sensual / sexual exploration with others is a part of that mix. Because this can be a "buzzy" issue, this conversation needs to take place well in advance of actually acting on it.

The likelihood is, as I mentioned above, your position on this will change over time.

Chapter Fourteen: Exercises in Elegant, Intimate Relating

Here's the ball plan. Now that you've read the book, (and your partner has too!) it's time to begin implementing what you learned.

Each of the Tools Needs Practice

Reread each of the Tools, and become more familiar with the ideas. Then, look for any exercises included in the section. Practice each of the Tools, all the time!

Now, take a bit of time to dissect what you've read.

Talk with your partner about your 'take' on what is required for Elegant, Intimate Relating. Which parts work for you? Which seem difficult, which seem impossible, and which do you disagree with? Are some ideas scary, or just plain weird?

After ample discussion time, decide what you are willing to commit to, right now. The 9 Tools are a good place to start – with the possible exception of some of the Exercises. Don't hold back from starting!

Devise a clear, "I" based statement – what you will commit to in your relationship, along with a statement asking your partner to hold you accountable for what you commit to.

The. Best. Relationship. Ever.

Example: *"I will always tell you the truth about me. Honesty is so important to me that if I lie to you, I would expect you to leave. And vice versa."*

This is diametrically the opposite of, "If you love me, you will not lie to me," or "I'll stop lying when you stop lying," or "Don't you know you shouldn't lie."

Another: *"I commit to 30 minutes a day of sitting with you and using the Communication Model to discover where we are in our relationship."*

Share your list with your partner and come to an agreement to proceed. What follows can then serve as a guide and resource for ideas.

Exercise # 1 – First Essay – Stages of Relating

This is a writing exercise. The goal is to answer the following questions, then share your answers with your partner. DO NOT edit your writing to fit what you think your partner wants to hear! Remember, we're all about honesty here!

Think back on the stages of your relationship.

Here's how it goes:

You meet, strike up a conversation, and decide you like someone. This leads to deciding to date. Now, as soon as you met, you both began to create data files, filled with bits of data. Initially, it's filled with "enchanting" bits–hormonally driven data about appearance, smell, what (s)he wears, how (s)he sounds. We could call this data, "The things about my new friend that turn me on."

- What were the things that first attracted you to your partner?

Exercises in Elegant, Intimate Relating

- What physical attributes turned you on? What were your expectations?
- What were your expectations about communication, truth telling, and intimacy with your partner?

As time goes by, biographical data is inserted, as are "likes and dislikes." Sexual preferences show up. Safe topics, unsafe topics, both appear as "do and don't" lists.

Making lists and engaging in meaning-making goes on when your partner is there, but more importantly, when (s)he is absent.

It is during the absences, especially, that you attached meaning to your partner's behaviour

You created a story and a judgement about who your partner is, and all of it was based upon your observations and interpretations. The meaning you attached was added by you, and is therefore only about you – it has absolutely nothing to do with your partner.

At some point, you toted up all of your beliefs, and decided you were ready for a commitment. Here's the irony: you committed to relating to the person you created in your head.

Jump ahead a few months, after the "commitment." At some point, the novelty wore off. You began to notice stuff that you had ignored.

- As time went by, when did you first notice you were judging your partner?
- What things did you dislike? How did you express your displeasure?

Typically, this is when the game-playing begins. You pulled out certain behaviours from your bag of tricks in an

The. Best. Relationship. Ever.

attempt to get your partner to change – to match the person you created in your head! Think about it. You created a person, in your head, and now you want the 'real person' to match your invention.

- What do you do to manipulate your partner?
- Which emotions do you 'pull out' to attempt to get your way? What is your favourite defensive statement, i.e. "That's not how I was brought up," or "No one else ever thought [did, acted,] that way with me?"
- What behaviours, in your partner, do you aggravate yourself over?

Take the time to really consider the image in your head, how it matches, and more important, how it does not match the 'present appearance' of your partner. Write it all down.

Now, pick a day or two to share what you wrote with your partner, following the Communication Model. No blaming, no defending. Listener, just listen. You may begin to see how things keep getting off the rails.

Then, without defense or comment, switch, and the other person reads what they wrote, while the other listens.

Exercise # 2 – Setting Aside Time

Set aside thirty minutes per day, for communication practice

No excuses! Many people tell me how busy their lives are, what with kids, work, shopping, TV watching, hockey, whatever. Their relationship sucks, but hey, "What do you expect? I don't have the time or energy for all this talking stuff. (S)he talks too much already!"

Exercises in Elegant, Intimate Relating

I expect 30 minutes a day of communication time from you. Or, go call your lawyer.

- 1) Pick a specific time and a specific location. Each person commits to showing up, every day, whether or not your partner is there. Live up to your commitment!
- 2) When partner shows up, each of you gets ten minutes to talk about whatever you choose. The very first thing to establish (each and every time) is what the speaker wants from the listener. There are really only three options:
  - I want you to listen.
  - I want you to listen and ask questions.
  - I want you to listen and offer suggestions.
- 3) Use the Communication Model!!! The pronoun of the authentic life is I. During this communication exercise, (and really, all the time) you must commit to speaking always and only for yourself, by using the pronoun, "I." "I think, I feel, I judge, the story I am telling myself ..." is key to elegant dialogue.
- 4) No matter what is said, it is the responsibility of the listener to listen, not to get defensive, make excuses, or explain. This exercise, which will go on day by day forever, provides a safe environment for each person to vent. What's being said isn't true or false. It's just words – and an entry-way into the mind of the speaker. There is nothing to defend.
- 5) After ten minutes (you may want to set a timer) the listener asks, "Do you want some feedback?" Ninety per cent of the time, the speaker would be wise to agree. Why? You have blind spots, and hearing about them is the first step to fixing them!
- 6) The "5-minute feedback" must not be in the form of a defense. It is a reflection on what the listener understood of the speaker's choice(s). For example, "So, I'm aware that you are angering yourself over this situation. I'm wondering why you're choosing that response."
- 7) Then, shift. The listener becomes the speaker, following the pattern, above.

The. Best. Relationship. Ever.

This differs from "normal" discussions in several ways:

- It's about dialogue, not about assigning blame.
- It's about self-exploration, not about making the partner responsible for fixing things.
- It's about learning to listen to complaints and blaming without biting.
- It's about listening to another's pain without rushing in to rescue.

Exercise # 3 – Resolving Issues

Having an Issue Conversation may have been, in the past, difficult for one or both of you. As in, "That's how the fights start!"

The more aware you are of what's happening between your partner's ears, the easier it will be to discuss issues. Clarity comes as we separate our defensiveness from the issue at hand. (see: "Being Self-Responsible")

- 1. Ask for, and set aside time, to talk about ONE issue.
- 2. Pick a name for the issue (something brief and to the point, like, "Designing a budget," or "Dinner with the in-laws."
- 3. Write the topic down on a pad of paper.
- 4. Do a quick, regular check in, using the Communication Model. (see item # 1, above.) The object is for each of you to state where your mind is, and how you are, before discussing the issue.
- 5. Now, turn to the issue. The person who suggested the issue goes first. Talk about it, from your perspective only, using the Communication Model. Flesh out the background story, your physical reactions, and especially the stories you tell yourself.
- 6. Partner, just listen. Then, as usual, ask for more depth: "Is there more you'd like to add? What else is up for you?"
- 7. Stop after 10 minutes.

- 8. Partner, do not address what your partner said. Rather, give your perspective on the issue, following the above guidelines, 5-6-7.
- 9. Now, each of you "mirror" (describe) what you heard your partner say.
- 10. Stop. Using paper, look for areas of agreement, and write them down. Look for areas of disagreement, and write them down. Start with the first disagreement, and discuss ways to work through the disagreement.
- 11. Remember, this is about the issue, NOT your partner! A disagreement is not personal. It is simply an issue to be resolved.
- 12. If either of you get into personalizing, as the other person notices, say, "It seems that you are raising another issue. Let's return to this issue, [pointing to the name for the issue you wrote in step # 2] and specifically to this item of disagreement."
- 13. If something comes up that either or both of you won't let go of, agree to add it to the "To be discussed later" list.

This approach keeps you on track and your emotions in check.

Exercise # 4 – Viewing another's World

For several years Dar and I have been offering what we call Weekend Residentials. It's an opportunity to move in with us for a weekend and to explore your issues. We provide dialogue, exercises, and bodywork as regular parts of this experience.

One of the exercises we assign couples is what we call the chair exercise. This is especially nice in good weather – lounge chairs outside are perfect – but the exercise can be done indoors also.

The. Best. Relationship. Ever.

One person sits in a comfortable lounge chair (or on a bed or couch) and leans against the back(board), with legs extended and spread. In a pinch you can sit on the floor, back against a wall, with a cushion under you. The other person sits between the open legs, back against chest.

Then the person in front talks.

The front person: describe what you are seeing (in the room or space in front of you) and how you interpret it. Or you can talk about your life, or your inner experience.

The person behind "just listens," and encourages the front person to keep sharing. The speaker speaks for 10 minutes, no interruptions.

Then change positions, and do the thing again. No feedback, no comments. This is a great way to make non-sensual / non-sexual physical contact and support while learning more about how the person in front processes their reality. Not right or wrong. Just listening to another person's experience.

Exercise # 5 – Implement a 'caring days' list

This exercise was devised by Richard B. Stuart, in his book, *"Helping Couples Change."*

First, take two pieces of paper. Put your name on the top of one of them, your partner's name on the other. Then, create a listing of the numbers 1 to 20, down the left side, leaving some space between each line.

Before we get to the exercise, let's differentiate between possible and impossible requests.

Exercises in Elegant, Intimate Relating

Impossible:

- Be nice to me (what's 'nice?')
- Make me happy (no one makes anyone anything.)
- Love me. (How?)
- Make me feel safe. (You make you safe.)
- Fix my problems. (You create your problems, and you fix them.)
- Don't demand things from me.
- Let me be me.
- Don't get mad.
- Never look at another (wo)man.

Possible:

- Give me a hug.
- Say "I love you," 3 times today.
- Give me a gentle neck rub.
- Ask me how my day was.
- Invite me to go for a 15 minute walk.
- Hold my hand in public.
- Take a shower with me.
- Give me a 15 minute cuddle.

Exercise:

- 1) On a blank piece of paper, list the Impossible Things you regularly expect from your partner. Share the lists with each other, and then burn the lists!
- 2) Take your number page that you just made. Create a Caring Days List. Each item on the list must be possible, positive (i.e.) "Rub my head," vs. "Don't ignore me," and do-able in 15 minutes or less. See above for suggestions. (There are additional suggestions online.)
- 3) You **may** list up to 20 behaviours. You **MUST** list at least 10.
- 4) Post your list.

The. Best. Relationship. Ever.

- 5) Read your partner's list. Commit to doing 5 items from the list, each day, for 30 days.
- 6) You do not have to do everything on the list. You must do at least 5 different ones each day.
- 7) You do your 5 no matter what your partner does!
- 8) Do this for at least a month.

Exercise # 6 – Establish a 'date night'

Amazing, really, how far "off the rails" most couples are. I've noticed that couples in trouble seldom if ever have dates with each other, let alone have "dirty weekends away."

Here come the excuses. "We're broke!" (Want to know how much that shiny, new divorce is going to cost?) "There's no time!" (Maybe after you're dead there will be more...) "We have kids!" (They'll survive without you for a few hours.) "What if we fight while we're on our date?' (Why the heck do you think you need a date in the first place? Get over yourself!)

Start out with a short (one hour) date, somewhere outside of the house, at least once a week. In Canada, there is huge chain of Donut Shops–Tim Horton's–we call them "Timmie's"–even a coffee date at Timmie's is preferable to nothing.

Or, pick a restaurant, and go there. Without the kids. Without friends. No distractions.

Learn to hang out again. After all, you used to hang out, didn't you? Go to free concerts in the park. Go for walks. Hold hands and talk. Go window shopping... only buy groceries instead ;-)

Exercise # 7 – Be sure you've set up a safe area for expressing emotions

Guess what? Emotions are a part of life. Not just the 'good' ones–all of them. You do not get to pick and choose which ones to have. You've got them all

We wrote about this in "Ways to express emotions." Here's the "plot" again, briefly.

We suggest:

- A safe space–an 8 x 8 area rug is about right.
- Get the furniture out of the way.
- No breaking stuff. No touching living beings. Words, pounding on a pillow, or a couch cushion, are all OK.
- 3-5 minute time limit to start, with repeats OK if everyone agrees.

Have a discussion about boundaries, and encourage each other to express anger, sadness, grief, disappointment, happiness, bliss. Be present with each other, and observe without comment.

Exercise # 8 – Essay 2 – write about your greatest fears

Another opportunity to write and share. We tend to be fairly protected around things we fear, especially if we are male. Women also fear stuff, and might be freer to express, but get caught in not wanting to get their partners going – as the men ride the white horse to the rescue.

Write about things you fear.

- What happens when you think about your death?
- Being alone – abandoned?
- Revealing the 'messy stuff' inside?

The. Best. Relationship. Ever.

- Being truly *seen* – many people have dreams of being naked in public – this is an indicator that one fears being 'really seen.'

What's on your list? Write about it, talk about it, using the above "back and forth" method.

No rescuing, fixing, jumping in, or judging allowed!!

Exercise # 9 – Silent sitting and eye-gazing

Here's one of those odd, chargy, scary things most people never do.

- Set it up this way: Sit opposite your partner, in a chair, a couple of feet apart. Set your timer for 5 minutes. Set it where you can't look at it.
- Breathe. Breathe throughout the exercise.
- Now, stare into your partner's eyes. Feel free to blink as you need to, and you will need to. Keep your focus on your partner's eyes. No looking away.
- If you do look away, just return your eyes to your partner's without comment.

At the end of 5 minutes, share your experience with your partner.

Exercise # 10 - Review the state of your relationship, and make a new commitment

By now, you're getting much better at listening and being revealing. This exercise is really the basis of your ongoing communication.

From now on, as you have your daily talk time, recognize that the real topic is 'the state of the union,' so to speak.

Exercises in Elegant, Intimate Relating

From now on, keep your partner in your loop. Share your thoughts, feelings, emotions.

Ask, specifically for what you want. Remember exercise # 5 – the Caring Days one. Remember to ask for what is possible, not for global, impossible things. Be a good communicator, using "I" language exclusively.

Pull out your commitment list from the beginning of this chapter, and review it, on your own time. See how well you are doing, and whether any of the items listed can use polishing. Re-write any ambiguous statements, and if something new has occurred to you, add it in.

Bring your list to a conversation time, read it to your partner, and re-commit to living, with integrity, **The. Best. Relationship. Ever.**

Chapter Fifteen: Sensual, Erotic Exercises

About the Exercises

The exercises below are described briefly. Some are linked to photos or videos that are available on this book's website.

The ideas presented below are hints and suggestions – if you find one or more interesting, do a Google search, and you'll find tons of articles, books and videos to guide you.

Other resources: search Google for "Sacred Intimate." There are professionals out there who do this work with individuals and couples.

Go to The Haven website [1], and then search for workshops led by Elfi Dillon Shaw. She teaches courses for women, and for partners.

Check the Body Electric site [2]. Elfi teaches there, too, and they offer one or two workshops a year for couples. It's where Dar and I first learned this work!

---

[1] www.haven.ca
[2] www.bodyelectric.org

Sensual, Erotic Exercises

Opening to Passion

I'm not going to get into a big discussion of the Chakras, but the energy we are working with in this chapter is "2nd Chakra" energy. The 2nd Chakra region surrounds the body, and includes the lower belly from the navel to the genitals, and the butt, including the sacrum.

We call the energy in this region "passion." On the back of the body side, it's passion for life – on the front of the body, sensual and sexual passion.

One of the first steps for releasing passionate energy (which includes creative, sensual, erotic, and sexual energy) is "keeping your knees apart and your pelvis loose."

Back Release

In this exercise, you'll discover how to loosen and unblock the 2nd Chakra (sacral and pelvic) region.

Find something round or half round to insert under the small of your back, placed *perpendicular* to your spine. Start with something small, like a rolled towel, and work up to a rolled blanket or a yoga bolster that might be six or 8 inches tall.

Let go. Let your lower back "melt" over the bolster – forming itself over the curve of the bolster. This requires a conscious action of "releasing." If your lower back tightens, breathe into the area, and let go again.

A yoga posture

Supta Bada Konasana (bound ankle pose) is the perfect posture for releasing the pelvis. The pose opens the groin and stretches the groin muscles, stretches and elongates the

The. Best. Relationship. Ever.

thigh muscles, and brings your attention fully to the 2nd Chakra Region of the body.

Lean back over a yoga bolster (or a rolled blanket) placed *parallel* to your spine, from under your head to the small of your back. Relax the small of your back – let it curve down, so that your butt touches the floor. Also relax your belly.

Your thighs are spread wide, and lying on their sides, knees touching the floor (if your knees don't touch the floor, support them with rolled-up blankets,) bent at the knees, and the soles of your feet are touching.

This opens the pelvis, and gets your knees wide apart. Relax, and breathe into your lower belly.

Intentional Dancing

This is a biggie – we do a lot of dancing in our workshops, and suggest it as a regular part of pelvic release work. There are two approaches. Experiment with both!

OSHO, the famous guru, created "active meditation," which we jokingly call "dancing until you drop." If you go to *Amazon*, and search "OSHO Active Meditation," you'll see several CD possibilities listed.

We especially recommend "Osho Kundalini Meditation." Buy the CD, and go for it!

The other approach uses music to practice moving your pelvis in all of the directions it goes:

- 1) It turns in a circle - think the Hula.
- 2) It rocks side-to-side - think salsa dancing.
- 3) It tips up and down (the pelvic tilt) - use your imagination!

There's music out there that is suitable for each of these three movements – Hawaiian, Latin, and "pelvic / hot."

The most neglected motion is the third one. In fact, this motion is so important that we teach it as a part of Breathwork – you learn to breathe, and then you learn to add a pelvic tilt. You can see a Breathwork explanation [3] on the online extras page. (The link is on the Resources page.)

Music: My buddy and editor Debashis Dutta recommends *"Leave Your Hat On,"* by Joe Cocker. I've never found a better song for the pelvic tilt than Alannah Myles' *"Black Velvet."* Download a copy, buy a copy, play it, and move your pelvis.

Sensuality Exercises

Most people never learn about sensuality – this being decidedly different from sexuality. Sensuality is conscious engagement with our senses – thus the word – and means that we revel in the pleasure that is entering us through our senses. All of them.

Belly Breathing

Spend time breathing into your lower belly. The directions for this are simple. Lay on your back, knees raised and slightly apart. Direct your attention to your lower belly, and specifically to the area 2 inches below your belly button. Breathe in, allowing your lower belly to expand and bulge out. Hold the breath for a count of 5, and then exhale forcefully and completely.

As you breathe, rub your belly in a clockwise circle, and deeply. The circle is from below your navel to above your pu-

---

[3] http://www.phoenixcentre.com/bodywork/body_language7.htm

The. Best. Relationship. Ever.

bic bone, between your pelvic bones. Do this directly on your skin.

Cuddling

As I mentioned above, many of my female clients mention the lack of "cuddling," which is a basic sensual activity. They crave sensual, or erotic, non-sexual contact, and when they try to get it, their partner often thinks it's an invitation to sex.

And many men find giving and receiving massage or non-sexual touch to be either uncomfortable or boring, and want to move past that.

So, we recommend setting up a "Cuddling Vulnerability Project."

Here's the description: Set up times for hugs and cuddles. Remind each other of your agreement: that the contact is not a prelude to sex. Instead, it's an opportunity to make deep physical contact, and to share your thoughts and feelings, as they arise.

Non-erotic, Sensual Massage

Perhaps one of the best ways to get into your body is to use massage. This is also a great "non-sexual" bonding exercise, as the Vulnerability Project "contract" is "massage only."

Buy a book or two on massage. I would especially recommend "*The New Massage: Second Edition*," by Gordon Inkeles. Using his book or others like it teaches what you need to know about sensual touch.

This massage, using oil, is about slow, medium pressure stroking of the body, as well as stretching the limbs, and stretching out the back. It differs from Erotic massage in that there is no massaging the anal / genital areas.

The strokes are like a deep caress, geared toward releasing tension, and discovering that simple touch "feels good."

The recipient should be blindfolded. As you receive this massage, notice when you are experiencing each sensation. If you find yourself leaving your body, and going into storytelling, breathe, let the story go, and come back to your experience.

Do the same if you notice you are tightening down muscles, especially your butt muscles. Breathe, wiggle, and let go.

Four-handed massage (non-erotic) – (see section on "Dialogue regarding physical contact with others.")

You need 2 friends for this one – the recipient is massaged by 2 people, thus 4-hands. Being massaged by more than one person is different from what one normally experiences. There is more contact, varied contact, and this equals more sensory - sensual input. The massage follows the guidelines just mentioned. It's best if the "massagers" keep their strokes coordinated throughout.

Practice full body hugging

This one may seem odd, but as therapist David Schnarch points out in his book, *"Passionate Marriage,"* most people are quite uncomfortable when hugging others, even their partners.

The. Best. Relationship. Ever.

Schnarch proposes a "project" he calls "Hugging 'till Relaxed," and describes it on his website [4]:

Try Hugging 'till Relaxed. Here's a terrific way to get more in touch with your partner while also getting a better grip on yourself. It turns a simple hug into a window into your relationship and a way to improve it. Prepare yourself by taking a few minutes to slow down, relax, and slow your heart rate. Then stand facing your partner a few feet away. Get a balanced, well-grounded stance over your own two feet. Close your eyes, take a breath, and relax again. Open your eyes, and when the two of you are ready, shuffle forward without losing your relaxed balanced position, so that you have one foot between your partner's feet. Get close enough that you can easily put your arms around your partner without feeling off balance, or pulling or pushing your partner off-balance either. Shift your stance or position as needed to be physically comfortable. Let yourself relax into the hug, and remember to breathe. Lots of feelings about your partner, your relationship and yourself are bound to surface. Note your resistances but don't give into them. Afterwords, talk about the experience with your partner. It often takes several months of practice, several times a week, but you'll be amazed by the many improvements this brings.

Practice hugging friends

Often, we limit our hugging to one or two people, Expand your repertoire to include good friends, and make a hugging agreement along the same lines as the above suggestion.

One thing to work on: drop the "A Frame" hugs – the ones where you're connected at the top and your pelvises are 2 feet apart. You don't have to "grind pelvises," but keeping them apart is a bit childish.

---

[4] ttp://www.passionatemarriage.com/ca_tips_for_more_passion.shtml

The Sitting Hug

Hugger, sit down on a couch, or the floor, and be sure that your back is fully supported, and that you are sitting on something soft. You want to be comfortable for multiple minutes.

Now, just sit there and invite the huggee to sit down, either next to you, or on your lap, or whatever the huggee wants.

Ask the huggee to make "herself" comfortable.

Huggee, wiggle a bit and find the posture that suits what you need. Once the position is comfortable for both of you, hugger, ask the huggee where "she" wants you to put your arms. Make no assumptions about anything.

Huggee, ask, specifically, for what you want. Oh. And make an agreement that it's OK to reposition yourselves as necessary, so that both of you remain comfortable throughout.

Eat a Rolo ®

I named this one in honour of an old friend's Rolo addiction. It's actually a "play" on the Mindful Eating exercise common to Zen. My friend was a Rolo ® fanatic, so I substituted the candy for an orange.

You can do a short version of this exercise by blindfolding the recipient, and slowly feeding the recipient a segment of orange / a piece of candy.

In the main exercise, you and your partner "partake" at the same time:

The. Best. Relationship. Ever.

- Each of you selects an orange. Set the orange down in front of you. Look at it. See how the light reflects off of it. Look at the colour, texture, and all the little pore-like thingies. Really look.
- Now, scrape your fingernail along the skin, and listen to the sound. Pierce the skin, and start peeling, and direct your attention to the sound of peeling, then to the sound of separating the segments.
- Go back to looking – seeing how the orange pieces look.
- Bring the skin to your nose, and smell it. Set it down. Bring a segment to your nose, and smell it. Give it a little squeeze and smell again.
- Squish one of the segments in your fingers, and really feel the pulp, juice, and any seeds or pith.
- Pop a segment into your mouth, and chew it slowly. See if you can take 5 minutes to eat one segment. Really taste it!
- Take another segment, and rub it on your arm or leg, or just get creative, and use your body to feel the orange section.
- Now, stop, and go either wash or hose off. (I'll wait until you get back...)

Think about and talk about your experience.

Be a Captive – Full Body Feeling

This is an interesting game that allows you to "play" with textures.

This massage requires that you gather supplies: For example, tactile: silk, feathers, loofah, leather, yarn balls, etc. Temperature: warm tea, ice, oil, etc. Food: chocolate sauce, honey, whipped cream, etc. The sky's the limit, so use your imagination.

Sensual, Erotic Exercises

You can add "captivity" to this exercise by lightly tying the recipient to a bed. Or, get a men's wooden suit coat hanger, hook it over a door, and have the recipient hold the bottom bar.

The recipient wears a blindfold, and the giver massages the recipient's body, first with the tactile substances.

The recipient "feels" the sensations of hard, soft, smooth, coarse, etc. The massage should be "whole body." A charge will likely build up as you experience how the items feel, and how the feeling shifts, depending on which part of the body is being massaged, by what.

Now, think temperature. When I do this exercise with clients, I often use warmed coconut oil, along with hot and cold massage stones.

You can also use "messy" things, like warm (not hot!) tea, Slurpees, (for the ice) and any liquid-y sauce you can imagine. Obviously, put down a tarp or drop cloth!!

(For ideas, check the movie *"9 1/2 Weeks,"* especially the scene with Mickey Rourke and Kim Basinger in front of the refrigerator...)

Exercises in Eroticism

I'm going to make some general comments about Erotic Massage, and then send you to a web link for specifics.

Erotic Massage

Erotic massage, like the other exercises, comes in flavours. There's a building process involved. The goal with erotic massage is to:

- 1) expand your physical / orgasmic responsiveness, and

The. Best. Relationship. Ever.

- 2) work at an intense bodily level that deepens orgasm without intercourse

The main "rule" is to work with someone you trust. You partner, ideally, and also search your area for "Sacred Intimates" if you are looking to work on this with a professional.

Another rule, in each of the massage exercises that follow, is that the recipient's knees should be *at least* 8-12 inches apart, and the belly and butt muscles should be "unclenched."

Level One

Non-genital erotic massage: Set up a space that is warm and comfortable. A massage table is great, but a bed or a pad on the floor works, too. You'll need massage oil (I like coconut oil, but it solidifies at about 74 degrees so you either need to warm it a bit or rub it around in your hands.)

Use long, sensuous strokes along the entire body, rubbing deeply but with restraint. In other words, you're caressing, not "fixing."

Recipient, focus on letting go and "turning on." You want to really, really enjoy this massage!

Work on the entire body, starting with the back, and working down to the butt and legs. The genital / anal region is the only area skipped. Spend some time working on the feet and hands.

On the front of the body, with little or no oil, caress the face. Then, with oil, work on the chest / breasts, nipples, belly and lower belly, and the front of the legs. Massage the genital / leg crease. Exclude the genitals.

Sensual, Erotic Exercises

End the massage by placing one hand on your partner's heart, the other on the lower belly. Hold this for a few minutes.

Level Two

Adding genital strokes: Believe it or not, there are many genital strokes to learn. With this massage, the goal is orgasm. (Men might search "Male Tantric practices" to learn how to separate orgasm from ejaculation – it makes for a "tidier" massage!)

This massage begins as above.

When you finish massaging the front of the body, instead of finishing with your hands on the belly and chest, you shift to Level 2 by placing one hand on the recipient's heart, and the other over his / her genitals. This is a grounding posture. Hold for a minute or two, and then begin the genital strokes.

This is important: this part of the massage requires dialogue. Once you have "run through" all of the strokes, the recipient chooses what (s)he likes. Everything is done "with permission."

Rather than attempt to describe the strokes and the process of the massage (as well as the musical selections (no, really!)) that go along with this process, here's a link to an amazingly detailed page, describing erotic massages for both men and women.

Read to the bottom of the page, as additional techniques are presented throughout.

http://www.sexuality.org/erotmass.html

The. Best. Relationship. Ever.

Learning to Feel and Move Energy

In Chinese thought, energy moves in the meridians. One Daoist practice is called the Microcosmic Orbit. I'll quote from Wikipedia first:

> *...in the microcosmic orbit meditation exercise Jing [energy] is encouraged to flow upwards along the Governor vessel during inhalation and then downwards along the conception vessel returning to the Dantian on the exhalation. This means that energy flows from the Dantian downwards to the base of the spine then up the back along the centre line of the body to the crown of the head, then over the head and down the front centre line of the body and back to the starting point again making a full circle or orbit....This raising and lowering Jing through the Microcosmic orbit and returning it to the Dantian purifies the essence and transforms it into Qi or vitality.*

Here's a description of how to do this.

- 1. Focus on your lower belly, 2 inches below your navel, and 2 inches in. [the lower Dantian] Breathe to this spot for a minute or so, and "feel" for the energy there (this is considered a major storehouse for energy.)
- 2. On an inhalation, imagine "dropping the energy" through your genitals, to your Root Chakra (base of the spine, perineum.) Imagine picking up energy from your genitals, and also "feel it" at the Root Chakra. As you do this, you might feel your perineum area throbbing, or pushing slightly outward.
- 3. Breathe deeply into your Root Chakra, (base of the spine area) for a few minutes.
- 4. Now, on an in breath, imagine drawing the energy up your spine (actually the Governing meridian.) The sensation is described as "sucking honey through a straw."
- 5. The energy travels up the spine. Imagine it moving up your neck and across your head. Touch the tip of your tongue to the roof of your mouth. This connects the Gov-

Sensual, Erotic Exercises

erning Vessel to the Conception Vessel [which runs down the front centre of your body.]
- 6. On an out breath, feel / direct the energy down your head, throat, and into your heart. Feel the energy in your heart – it becomes lighter.
- 7. Breathe once more, and push the energy from your heart back into your lower belly.
- 8. Now breathe slowly, and imagine the entire cycle happening with each breath.
- 9. Remember to keep your tongue touching the roof of your mouth until your finish the exercise.

As a variation, as you are learning this, your partner can massage the areas in order: lower belly, genitals, perineum, spine, neck, head, neck, center of chest, center of upper belly, back to lower belly.

You don't have to believe any of this to feel it. Darbella teaches this practice as part of her Qi Gong trainings, and I often touch the points described above in Bodywork. Just do it and see.

Knowing what your energy feels like will aid the next exercise!

The Yab Yum Posture

In Tantra, this posture is well known. It too comes in flavours.

The posture is possible for any couple, same sex or opposite. The only "fiddling" necessary is if one partner is appreciably taller than the other – in this case, the taller person of either sex might sit in the bottom position.

To make the verbal description easier, I'll assume a taller male, and opposite sex couple.

The. Best. Relationship. Ever.

For levels one, two, and three, both parties can wear clothing on the lower half of the body.

Level One: The man sits on the floor, legs apart. The woman sits on the floor, perhaps a foot away, and places her legs over the man's, so they are "thigh to thigh." The genitals are lined up, but not in contact. The woman lightly encircles the man's lower back with her legs.

Both partners – reach forward with your left hand, and place it over your partner's heart. Then place your right hand over your partner's hand, on your own chest.

Look into your partner's eyes. Coordinate breathing. Imagine a flow of energy between the two of you. Breathe and look, for 5 minutes or so.

Level Two: The woman slides forward, so genitals are touching. Butts remain on the floor. The man wraps his legs lightly around the woman's lower back.

The breath becomes a circle. The woman breathes in and imagines the energy flowing from her genitals, up the front of the body, then out the heart on the out breath.

The man breathes in, imagining energy entering his heart and flowing down the front of his body to his genitals, and exiting his genitals on the out breath.

Level Three: The woman sits on the man's thighs, which are crossed under her. The genitals are in contact. The hands no longer are on each other's hearts, but rather wrapped around the partner. Again, make eye contact and imagine the flow of energy, as above.

Level four: see sexuality section

Erotic four-handed Massage

As described above, four-handed massage adds in another person – a great way to get over erotic shyness. The two people massage the third, and the recipient determines "go / no go" areas.

This is an oil massage, and the two "givers" are best to coordinate their strokes. It feels more balanced that way. Through discussion and permission giving, the "massagers" include the anal / genital areas into the massage.

This differs from classical erotic massage in that there is no emphasis on the myriad genital strokes, but rather making erotic contact with the genitals as part of the larger massage experience.

Sexuality

You'll notice much emphasis in this section on making time and taking the opportunity for physical contact - slow physical contact. In this section I want to just make a few brief suggestions for developing your sexuality through intentional contact.

Sexual Healing

Most of us learned about sex as I described it above: "in the back seat." We may have had a lot of practice with intercourse, but precious little feedback.

The other thing to remember is every person is different. This was an obvious lesson at the erotic massage training event Darbella and I attended. Every person responded differently – very differently.

The. Best. Relationship. Ever.

You learned to ask, you learned to listen, and you learned to be flexible.

Spend some teaching time: On a regular basis, take the time to teach your partner what you like. One of the key retraining exercises therapists suggest (devised, if I remember correctly, by Masters and Johnson) is what might be called the sitting spooning position.

One partner sits on the bed, back against the headboard, legs spread. Their partner backs into the space between the legs, and places "her" back against "his" chest.

The "rules" are: this exercise is not to lead to intercourse, and the person in the front directs all of the action. Person in front, take your partner's hands in yours, and teach your partner how to touch your chest / breasts, nipples, and genitals. Person in back, don't rush! Follow your partner's lead. Ask questions about pressure, speed, duration. Be curious!

This is a perfect way to help one's partner to know how the person in front wants to be touched, and where, and how. The exercise should take 30 minutes or so. Take a break, then switch.

Yab Yum, level 4

The only difference from levels 1 - 3 is complete nudity, and penetration.

Assume the same posture as Level Three. Same breathing pattern: woman breathes in energy (in breath) through her genitals, up her body, and out her heart (out breath). Man receives energy through his heart (in breath) and breathes it down his body, and out his genitals on the out breath.

Chapter Sixteen: Reflection – What's Next

Endless reflection

Back in the section on the Communication Model, I included a short paragraph on "Reflection" – the act of consciously monitoring your intention as compared to your behaviour.

I want to say here that Reflection, as well as all of the ideas presented in this book, require diligent effort. Darbella and I have been in relationship since 1982, and I notice that I still want to revert back to ways of being that get me lousy results.

It's the endless reflection that keeps this from happening

The more invested I am in being right, or blaming Dar, or blaming the situation, the more deeply I want to revert. I want to win, to punish, to control. I spent the first 32 years of my life doing exactly that, and my Ego loved every moment of it.

My Ego continues to nag me, and will until I die. It wants me to do what I used to do. Even though I've shifted my non-helpful behaviour for 30 years (as of 2012,) my Ego still resists.

The. Best. Relationship. Ever.

Your Ego will too

One of my favourite clients said, "I just want this to be over, and I never want to hurt myself and others again."

I replied, "We always have a choice of what we do next, but there is no way to "just stop" – there is no cure for our Egos."

Thus, this book isn't a quick fix, or even a fix at all. It's a skill set. And like any other skill, your elegance improves with practice.

However, and it's a big however, the better you get at something, the more likely it is you'll confront even more difficult situations – things that test your mettle – that call to you, "It's OK! Ream him / her a new one! This time, it's deserved!"

It's why I've encouraged you to get to know how you tighten your body

You want to find the physical signs that you are about to go off the rails, so that, as soon as you feel "tight," you can stop and have a breath, re-think your intentions regarding Elegant, Intimate Relating, and immediately go back to your new behaviour(s).

I call this learning to "watch"

The signs are apparent – right here, right now, all the time. As we engage with each other, we can't help but signal our intentions, our feelings, and our level of resistance. The wise soul is paying attention in two directions.

Sensual, Erotic Exercises

First, you notice what is going on for you

Where are you tight / loose? What seems 'good,' what seems 'bad?' What physical sensations are you experiencing? These are all things that you report to your partner, as they are occurring.

Once you "notice" what you're doing, start shifting behaviours.

- If you notice that you are talking loud and fast, shift to talking quietly and slowly.
- You may notice that you've been talking non-stop for 10 minutes, so stop and ask your partner, "And what's going on for you?"
- If you're tucked into a ball, try uncrossing your crossed parts, sitting with your feet on the floor, knees apart, and uncross your arms. See what happens.
- If emotions are arising that threaten to be directed at another, use the techniques from "Ways to Express Emotions" to direct them at an inanimate object.
- If you are noticing you want to blame, fight, provoke, or slink off and hide (the infamous "silent treatment,") breathe, stay put, and report in, then return to the Communication Model.

Second, you observe your partner

Clearly and nonjudgementally see things like muscles tightening, leaning away or drawing closer, arms and legs crossing or uncrossing. Are his eyes focussed on you, or looking away, undiscussed? Is she fiddling with her clothing?

In other words, what you focus on is what you see, hear (tone of voice, not content), etc.

Example: A client said, "I want to talk about orgasms." As she did, she crossed her arms across her chest, and crossed

The. Best. Relationship. Ever.

her legs at her knees and ankles. I grinned, pointed to her arms and legs, then opened my hands, while raising my eyebrows. No interpretation necessary!!

She said, "Geez, I guess I really do a number on myself. No wonder I have issues with this."

Remember, it's not your job to *interpret* what you see your partner doing. Just be curious. "So, I notice you're leaning away and wringing your hands, and I'm wondering what's going on for you?" There are no hard and fast rules – other than to notice, and then to express this by being curious.

"I notice that you're [whatever you notice] and I'm wondering if you're aware you're doing that, and what's up for you?"

Final Thoughts

I know. You might be feeling a bit of overwhelm right now. All of this is so different from your norm, and different from the norm for others too.

I want you to know that, with persistent practice, the language of self-responsibility becomes second nature. The use of the Communication Model becomes easy and assured. Curiosity becomes your watch-word, and judgements and the need to be right falls away.

With practice

If Elegant, Intimate Relating is what you want, you can have it. Starting right now, and for the rest of your life.

Moment by moment, decision by decision, interaction by interaction.

Sensual, Erotic Exercises

What you are doing isn't working, and this does. So, really, what are you waiting for?

Resources

This section contains links to my other books, to items and places I mentioned in the book, and contact information should you have questions.

Half Asleep in the Buddha Hall

Wayne's "Eastern" book takes you by the hand and leads you to Zen-based peace of mind. *Half Asleep in the Buddha Hall* is a Zen based guide to living life fully and deeply. Using Zen stories old and new, as well as other illustrations and exercises, Wayne C. Allen takes you on an adventure into the uncharted territory of yourself.

Living Life in Growing Orbits

Living Life in Growing Orbits is designed to help you actually enact ideas such as:

- finding your limiting beliefs
- opening your mind, heart, and soul
- learning to speak with clarity and directness

Living Life in Growing Orbits is designed to be read and worked through, day-by-day, over an entire year:

Each week begins with a vital concept – written in a simple and engaging style designed to get you to think about what you believe. Following the weekly thought are exercises for the next seven days – things to do, to write about, to think about, and emphatically, to practice. Each vital concept is paired to its opposite, and each leads to the next, in a carefully designed building process.

Understandings flow intuitively and naturally, as you experiment with a shift of behaviours to match your new understandings.

This Endless Moment

Worthwhile change comes at a price. If you're tired of the same old relationships, the same situations cropping up again and again, and you find yourself stuck in the middle, then right now, you can do something about it! It's time to decide!

If you are willing to commit to living the life you have dreamed of, surrounded by meaningful and deep relationships, while making a real difference in the world, you need This Endless Moment.

Find Your Perfect Partner

Back in 1999, I wrote a booklet called "The List of 50." Part of a series of free booklets on aspects of relationships, "The List" was a guide to deciding whom you want to be in relationship with, and then putting what you decide into action.

My clients, since then, have asked me to expand upon this concept of conscious dating. So, I re-wrote the booklet into a 100 page book. In addition to completely revising the structure and contents of the booklet, I have included comments from readers, as well as sample Lists of 50. If you'd

The. Best. Relationship. Ever.

like to know more about this great resource, head over to our website. From there you can read a sample and order the book!

Resources for this book

Extra Resource page:

http://www.phoenixcentrepress.com/the-best-relationship-ever/resources-for-the-best-relationship-ever/

The Phoenix Centre Press website, home of my books:

http://www.phoenixcentrepress.com/

Our amazing blog, *The Pathless Path*

http://www.phoenixcentre.com/blog/

Wayne C. Allen is the web's Simple Zen Guy.
Wayne was born in Buffalo, New York in January of 1951.
His interest in psychology led him to Elmhurst Illinois, where he completed a B. A. in (1973).
He immigrated to Ontario, Canada in 1975.
Wayne received a Master's in Pastoral Counselling (M.Th.) in 1983, from Wilfrid Laurier University, Waterloo, Ontario.

Wayne retired in 2013, after 31 years as a psychotherapist.

He is the author of several books, all counselling/Zen related.

Wayne's approach to writing, life, and living comes from his love of Zen. His emphasis is on living in the now, and taking full responsibility for "how everything goes." His books are written in easy to understand language, and his insights are fresh and to the point. Wayne emphasizes wholeness, peace, and clarity of thought.

You can read more about them at Amazon, or at Wayne's publishing site, The Phoenix Centre Press. (http://www.phoenixcentrepress.com)

In his spare time he's a painter and photographer.

Wayne and Darbella are now travelling the world, teaching, learning, and enjoying "retirement."

www.ingramcontent.com/pod-product-compliance
Lightning Source LLC
Chambersburg PA
CBHW070646160426
43194CB00009B/1606